A very special thank you to John Barrett Hughes and Kim Pillsbury, for all your support, encouragement, and patience with me during this process. And a thank you to the best video editor a gal can have, Shelby Pollack.

In honor of my Big Brother, you are missed.
I dedicate this to his children, my niece, Samantha and my nephew, Patrick.
I will love and support you both the best that I can.

Hello!

I've been relying on some sort of coping skill since the age of six after the death of a family member which can only be described as horrific. By first grade I was suffering with severe anxiety. A school psychologist along with a ton of support helped me build ways to calm myself, so I stopped seeing the school nurse for those "tummy aches" I suffered.

From pictures of living and those who have passed on my desk. To carrying a worry stone with me, I found ways to cope. Together we did everything we could to help calm my tiny head of those racing thoughts.

I am now a Licensed Professional Counselor, a Nationally Certified Counselor, a Certified Grief Professional, and Yoga Alliance Certified RYT 200. Entering the world of mental health as a practitioner in my mid-twenties I found myself on a whole new path to coping. Starting in the world of cognitive behavioral techniques, I then traveled into the world of mindfulness, distress-tolerance, and self-soothing techniques in my early thirties. Eventually, landing in the world of energy and bodywork practices in my mid to late thirties.

With these skills and modalities, I have had the pleasure of providing psycho-education presentations on mindset, emotional eating habits, body image, coping with aging parents, trauma-education, and grief and loss. In 2019 I released my first workbook, Food, Mood, and You.

Since fall of 2020 I have further explored bodywork as a means of healing. I became a breath work facilitator and a certified yoga instructor. In the fall of 2021 my wellness company and I, Let Go Let Be, launched its first grief workshop, a full day of experiential healing. Incorporating these techniques in grief and trauma work with my clients has helped them reconnect to their physical bodies and emotions.

This collection of knowledge and education has been used in the development of the 52 skills you are about to experience. This workbook was created for you, the overwhelmed working parent, the anxious teenager, the depressed college freshman, the stressed-out businessperson, and the confused 30-something learning to navigate life.

After nearly two decades of working in the mental health field I found one commonality amongst the individuals I work with, a need for coping skills. As a therapist I set out to bring my clients tangible skills to use when feeling upset. I tell them, "I like to know you have 2 or 3 good skills in your back pocket." I hope this workbook fills both of your back pockets!

Best Wishes,

Tara Arhakos, MS, LPC, NCC, CGP

Find out more at:
www.mindfulmomentsllc.com
@TaraArhakos
www.youtube.com/@LetGoLetBe

Each week you will be presented with a new skill to practice. You can choose to pick any skill within the book or go in order with the book. These skills are intended to be easily accessible and applicable because who needs complicated tasks when you are already having a moment. Do not wait to be upset to use the skill. I mean come on! How realistic is it to pull out a skill that seems odd and maybe uncomfortable when you are already having a hard time? So, try the skill shortly after reading about it and just practice it.

Try the skill out three times. Why? Well, honestly because I'm corny and believe after three times you will have a better grasp on the skill and a more accurate opinion if it is a skill for you. Listen, not every skill is made for every person. I love the idea of mindful meditation, but the truth is it is a challenge for me and not always my most useful skill.

At the end of each week, you will find a review page. This is intended to help you assess the usefulness, difficulty, and applicability of the skill. Usefulness and difficulty are rated on a 1 - 7 scale, 7 indicating the highest level of usefulness or difficulty and 1 indicating not useful or very difficult. You can also assess the pros and cons of the skills, your overall mood for the week, and any other thoughts, feelings, or reactions to the skill. The Woo-Hoo of the week is a place to record something you are proud of regarding yourself or acknowledging something you did well for the week.

TABLE OF CONTENTS

- **Calm Yourself - Self Soothing Skills**   Page
  - Skill 1 -Four Square Breathing   1
  - Skill 2 - Go Back to Your Childhood   3
  - Skill 3 - Personal Mantra   6
  - Skill 4 - Breath of Fire   9
  - Skill 5 - Shout it Out   13
  - Skill 6 - Be in Nature   16
  - Skill 7 - High-Five Calm-Down   19

- **Feel Your Feelings - Emotional Regulation Skills**
  - Skill 1 - "I Feel Because" Journaling Activity   22
  - Skill 2 - Body Scan Meditation   26
  - Skill 3 - Sit With It   29
  - Skill 4 - What is Your Body Telling You?   32
  - Skill 5 - Early Warning Signs   35
  - Skill 6 - Understanding Anger   39
  - Skill 7 - Find Your Wise Mind   44

- **Be Positive - Encouragement & Organizational Skills**
  - Skill 1 - Daily Grinds & Gratitude   50
  - Skill 2 - Tada List   53
  - Skill 3 - Affirmations   56
  - Skill 4 - Flip it to the Positive   60
  - Skill 5 - Chart it Out   63
  - Skill 6 - Surprise Greeting Cards   67
  - Skill 7 - The Gratitude Jar   69

TABLE OF CONTENTS

- **<u>Change Your Thoughts - Cognitive Techniques</u>** **Page**
  - <u>Skill 1 - End Stinking Thinking</u> 71
  - <u>Skill 2 - 3-Minute Catastrophe</u> 74
  - <u>Skill 3 - Thought Dumping</u> 77
  - <u>Skill 4 - Box of Expectations</u> 81
  - <u>Skill 5 - Throw Out the Crystal Ball</u> 85
  - <u>Skill 6 - Thought Reframing</u> 88
  - <u>Skill 7 - The Two Week Rule</u> 93
  - <u>Skill 8 - Make it Absurd</u> 95

- **<u>Be Present and Mindful - Mindfulness & Grounding Techniques</u>**
  - <u>Skill 1 - Describe 5 Things</u> 98
  - <u>Skill 2 - Enhancing Your Mindfulness</u> 101
  - <u>Skill 3 - Plant Your Feet</u> 105
  - <u>Skill 4 - The Power of Sound Healing</u> 108
  - <u>Skill 5 - Root to Rise Grounding</u> 111
  - <u>Skill 6 - Intentional Movement</u> 113
  - <u>Skill 7 - Learn to Surrender Journaling Activity</u> 116
  - <u>Skill 8 - 5,4,3,2,1 Grounding</u> 120

TABLE OF CONTENTS

- **Be Kind to Yourself and Others - Self-Compassion & Acceptance Techniques** — Page
  - Skill 1 - Letters of Gratitude — 123
  - Skill 2 - My Best Self — 125
  - Skill 3 - Self-Esteem & Self-Praise — 129
  - Skill 4 - A Letter of Self-Praise — 133
  - Skill 5 - Hugs for a Smile — 135
  - Skill 6 - Letter to Your Younger Self — 137
  - Skill 7 - Self-Talk — 141
  - Skill 8 - Letter of Forgiveness — 145

- **Self-Care - Maintenance & Relapse Prevention Skills**
  - Skill 1 - Finding Balance — 149
  - Skill 2 - Self-Care on a Budget — 154
  - Skill 3 - Social Support Inventory — 158
  - Skill 4 - Take Five — 164
  - Skill 5 - The Pro's & Con's — 167
  - Skill 6 - Laugh Your Way to Chill — 170
  - Skill 7 - Healing Environment — 173

- **Appendix**
  - Script for Breath of Fire — 179
  - Script for Body Scan Meditation — 181
  - Script for What Your Body is Telling You? — 186
  - End Stinking Thinking - Unhelpful Styles of Thinking — 188
  - Script for Root to Rise Grounding — 191

CALM YOURSELF

SELF-SOOTHING SKILLS

FOUR SQUARE BREATHING

One of the easiest to remember and one of my personal go-to skills is Four Square Breathing.

- **Inhale while counting to 4 in your head.**
- **Hold your breath for a count of 4.**
- **Exhale for a count of 4 (challenge yourself to really lengthen this exhale).**
- **Breathe normal for a count of 4 and just reconnect to any sensations in your body.**

<u>Repeat as needed</u>

Use four square breathing as frequent and as necessary. It is easy to do in the car, a business meeting, or a long line at the grocery store. If you forget one part, like I often forget to hold my inhale, just keep going. You'll get the pattern down in the next round of breaths. Work on extending that exhalation as it signals the parasympathetic nervous system to calm the body down, which will leave you feeling lighter and grounded at the end of your breath work. **Head over to our YouTube Channel at <u>www.youtube.com/@LetGoLetBe</u> for a guided recording of this skill.**

Benefits:
- *Enhances blood flow.*
- *Stimulates the vagus nerve (which is the light switch to the "fight or flight" system).*
- *Improves sleep.*
- *Detoxes the body by improving the lymphatic system, decreasing inflammation, and releasing other toxins from the body through exhalations.*

REVIEW

PROS OF THIS WEEK'S SKILL

____

____

____

CONS OF THIS WEEK'S SKILL

____

____

____

WOO – HOO OF THE WEEK

____

____

____

____

REACTIONS TO THIS WEEK'S SKILL

____

____

____

____

____

____

____

____

DIFFICULTY OF SKILL

(1) (2) (3) (4) (5) (6) (7)

USEFULNESS OF SKILL

(1) (2) (3) (4) (5) (6) (7)

OVERALL MOOD THIS WEEK

NOTES

____

GO BACK TO YOUR CHILDHOOD

Go back to your childhood this week. This week you will consider the activities you enjoyed as a child and try implementing two of these activities or finding something like them in the present day.

Often when we are at a loss for what will calm us down and ground us, we miss the obvious. Going back to an activity you enjoyed as a child can be extremely soothing and familiar during times of distress. These activities were typically pleasurable, entertaining, and comforting all of which are needs that you continue to have throughout your life span.

These activities do not have to be extraordinary. In fact, it is best if they are simple and easily accessible for you.

GO BACK TO YOUR CHILDHOOD

CHILDHOOD ACTIVITIES

- Coloring
- Play a card game
- Play with play-dough
- Puzzles
- Make a collage
- Listen to a story
- Draw
- Jump rope
- Go for a bike ride
- Roller skate
- Dance to your favorite song
- Hula Hoop
- Play with sand
- Play a board game
- Paint
- Write a short story
- Play with silly putty
- Go swimming
- Read a book

WHAT DID YOU LOVE TO DO?

WEEKLY

REVIEW

PROS OF THIS WEEK'S SKILL

____

____

____

CONS OF THIS WEEK'S SKILL

____

____

____

WOO – HOO OF THE WEEK

____

____

____

____

REACTIONS TO THIS WEEK'S SKILL

____

____

____

____

____

____

____

DIFFICULTY OF SKILL

(1) (2) (3) (4) (5) (6) (7)

USEFULNESS OF SKILL

(1) (2) (3) (4) (5) (6) (7)

OVERALL MOOD THIS WEEK

NOTES

____

____

PERSONAL MANTRA

This week you will either build your own personal mantra or find one that resonates with you.

After doing so put this into practice! Ideally use it as much as you can but of course try to use it at least three times throughout the week to see what reaction you have to it.

Mantras are used to help promote mindfulness. Mindfulness is the practice of remaining present in the moment without judgment of oneself, others, or the situation, while practicing radical acceptance.

The purpose behind a mantra is to pull the mind and body back into the present moment. Mantras are not always just statements. A mantra could be a sound you make that helps reconnect to your body and mind.

My personal mantra is "let go, let be." This came to me after struggling for years to stay present during yoga classes. I would repeat it to myself every time I found my mind wandering from my yoga practice.

Benefits:
- *Alleviates ruminating thoughts when you feel like your mind is on a merry go-round.*
- *Reduces anxiety associated with obsessive thinking patterns.*
- *Teaches you how to redirect your mind and thoughts.*

PERSONAL MANTRA

PERSONAL MANTRA

- I am brave and can conquer my fears every day.

- It is what it is.

- I trust my body and mind with ease.

- I am capable.

PERSONAL MANTRA

REVIEW

PROS OF THIS WEEK'S SKILL

____

____

____

CONS OF THIS WEEK'S SKILL

____

____

____

WOO – HOO OF THE WEEK

____

____

____

____

REACTIONS TO THIS WEEK'S SKILL

____

____

____

____

____

____

____

____

DIFFICULTY OF SKILL

① ② ③ ④ ⑤ ⑥ ⑦

USEFULNESS OF SKILL

① ② ③ ④ ⑤ ⑥ ⑦

OVERALL MOOD THIS WEEK

NOTES

____

BREATH OF FIRE

Breath of Fire should NOT be performed if you are pregnant, suffer from high blood pressure or cardiac issues, have any respiratory infections, suffer from vertigo or spinal issues. If any of the fore-mentioned conditions apply, please do NOT perform this exercise and return to practicing Four Square breathing from Calm Yourself, Skill 1, page 1 or try The Body Scan Meditation found in Feel Your Feelings, Skill 2, page 26.

This week you will be performing a form of pranayama breathing, or yogic breath work called Breath of Fire. <u>Follow the guided meditation included in the appendix on page 180</u> or you can find a recording of this meditation on our YouTube Channel at <u>www.youtube.com/@LetGoLetBe</u> .

- **This breath work takes place in the diaphragm creating a pumping sensation from this area.**
- **By rapidly inhaling and exhaling from the lungs you will create a rhythm to your breathing.**
- **Breath of Fire creates a warming sensation within you, which releases toxins from the body.**

Fair warning – this feels weird and foreign at first. It does take some practice. If you lose the rhythm just slowly work back into it. As a beginner this rhythm can be slower, it is more important to find the rhythm and groove than to force the rapid pace commonly seen in Breath of Fire.

Practicing this breath work a few times over the next week can help you build the skill and become more comfortable with it. The more experience you get with this, the more you may see how it can be beneficial to your everyday self-care.

BREATH OF FIRE

If it turns out the Breath of Fire isn't for you, no worries. Not every skill is going to be for you but use the weekly review to see how this skill may or may not be your breath of choice!

Benefits:
- *Stimulates the Vagus Nerve so it can have both a calming and energizing effect.*
- *Boosts brain function.*
- *Releases toxins from the body.*
- *Improves respiratory functioning.*
- *Improves digestive functioning.*

BREATH OF FIRE

- How would you describe your experience with this breath work?

- What parts did you find challenging?

- Did you find yourself feeling energized or calmer afterwards? If so, what did this feel like for you?

- Could you see this breath work becoming part of your coping mechanisms?

WEEKLY

REVIEW

PROS OF THIS WEEK'S SKILL

____

____

____

CONS OF THIS WEEK'S SKILL

____

____

____

WOO – HOO OF THE WEEK

____

____

____

____

REACTIONS TO THIS WEEK'S SKILL

____

____

____

____

____

____

____

____

DIFFICULTY OF SKILL

(1) (2) (3) (4) (5) (6) (7)

USEFULNESS OF SKILL

(1) (2) (3) (4) (5) (6) (7)

OVERALL MOOD THIS WEEK

NOTES

____

SHOUT IT OUT

Let's get primal this week! This week you will be using your voice to help release feelings of anger, frustration, or anxiety by screaming out loud or singing at the top of your lungs.

- **Find a safe and comfortable place.**
- **Scream, sing, sigh, shout . . . GET LOUD!**
- **Then process the emotions you released. Processing is crucial. It can be the catalyst to change.**

After releasing that initial tension find a method to help you process the stressor and feelings around the stressor. You may choose to free write in a journal, maybe write a letter to the person that's involved if that seems fit (it will probably be one of those letters you never send). Give yourself the free range to explore what is upsetting you. Try this technique out a couple of times and you may find different methods of primal release or methods of processing that better fit you.

SHOUT IT OUT

Benefits:
- *Reduces stress, tension, anger, frustration, and anxiety.*
- *The vibrational frequency from using your voice can unlock stagnant and stubborn energies from within the body.*
- *Screaming can mimic the endorphins released through exercise leaving you with a sense of relief and provide an energy boost.*
- *Singing lowers cortisol levels, better known as the stress hormone.*

<u>Shout It Out Example:</u>
- **Singing in your car with the music blasting so loudly that you can feel the emotions coming out of you and maybe even tears.**
- **Letting out the loudest scream you can while on an empty beach. Just yell it out to the ocean and allow mother nature to take your pain.**

REVIEW

PROS OF THIS WEEK'S SKILL

____

____

____

CONS OF THIS WEEK'S SKILL

____

____

____

WOO – HOO OF THE WEEK

____

____

____

____

REACTIONS TO THIS WEEK'S SKILL

____

____

____

____

____

____

____

____

DIFFICULTY OF SKILL

(1) (2) (3) (4) (5) (6) (7)

USEFULNESS OF SKILL

(1) (2) (3) (4) (5) (6) (7)

OVERALL MOOD THIS WEEK

NOTES

____

BE IN NATURE

One of the easiest ways to reconnect to oneself is through being in nature.

Find your preferred outdoor space. Some may prefer to be by the water, some may love nothing more than to be up in the mountains, or at a nearby park. Even if your only option is your very own backyard, give yourself the opportunity to experience it today like it's the first time you've ever discovered this place.

Take ten minutes and simply observe and describe what you see. Describing the scenery in detail but without judgement. So, those flowers your partner planted that normally you can't stand just notice them as they are without any judgment. Notice their colors, the design of their petals, the texture of their leaves, take in all that you can without labeling them as good, bad, ugly, or beautiful. Enjoy these few minutes of tranquility!

BE IN NATURE

Benefits:
- *Boosts mood from sun exposure and vitamin D production.*
- *Helps refocus those tired and strained eyes from spending hours on electronics.*
- *Improved sleep due to melatonin production from sun exposure.*
- *Improved relationships when spending time outdoors with friends and loved ones.*
- *Increase in mindfulness practice which contributes to a sense of peace and acceptance.*
- *Mindfulness decreases ruminating thought patterns, anxiety, and worry.*
- *Reduction in stress from walking or sitting outdoors.*

Be In Nature Example:
- I <u>see</u> the brown bark on the tree splitting from the bottom of the trunk of the tree.
- I <u>hear</u> leaves rustling above my head.
- I can <u>feel</u> the sun warming up the skin on my cheek as its bright yellow rays shine towards me.
- I <u>feel</u> the cool air blow against my face.
- I <u>see</u> the clouds gliding across the bright blue sky.

REVIEW

PROS OF THIS WEEK'S SKILL

____

____

____

CONS OF THIS WEEK'S SKILL

____

____

WOO – HOO OF THE WEEK

____

____

____

____

REACTIONS TO THIS WEEK'S SKILL

____

____

____

____

____

____

____

DIFFICULTY OF SKILL

(1) (2) (3) (4) (5) (6) (7)

USEFULNESS OF SKILL

(1) (2) (3) (4) (5) (6) (7)

OVERALL MOOD THIS WEEK

NOTES

____

HIGH-FIVE CALM-DOWN

This next skill is another oldie but goodie. And it fits right in your pocket so you can use it anywhere and at any time. The high-five calm-down method helps distract you from negative thoughts and redirects you to the present moment.

Here's how it works. Each finger represents something different for you to recall or name.

High-Five Calm-Down:
- **Thumb: Name one thing you are proud of yourself for.**
- **Pointer finger: Point to something in nature.**
- **Middle finger: Name one person you are grateful for.**
- **Ring finger: Name a time you felt loved.**
- **Pinky finger: Name something you are looking forward to.**

During moments of anxiety or even sadness this quick skill can help ground you and perk-up your mood. Your responses may vary when you use this or you may find some of them to be the same, either way it's okay! Be sure to try this one out a few times. And practice it when you aren't upset so that it is easier to recall when you are in need.

Quick Tip
This method works great when you are stuck in bumper-to-bumper traffic and feeling frustrated and overwhelmed.

HIGH-FIVE CALM-DOWN

QUICK REFERENCE GUIDE

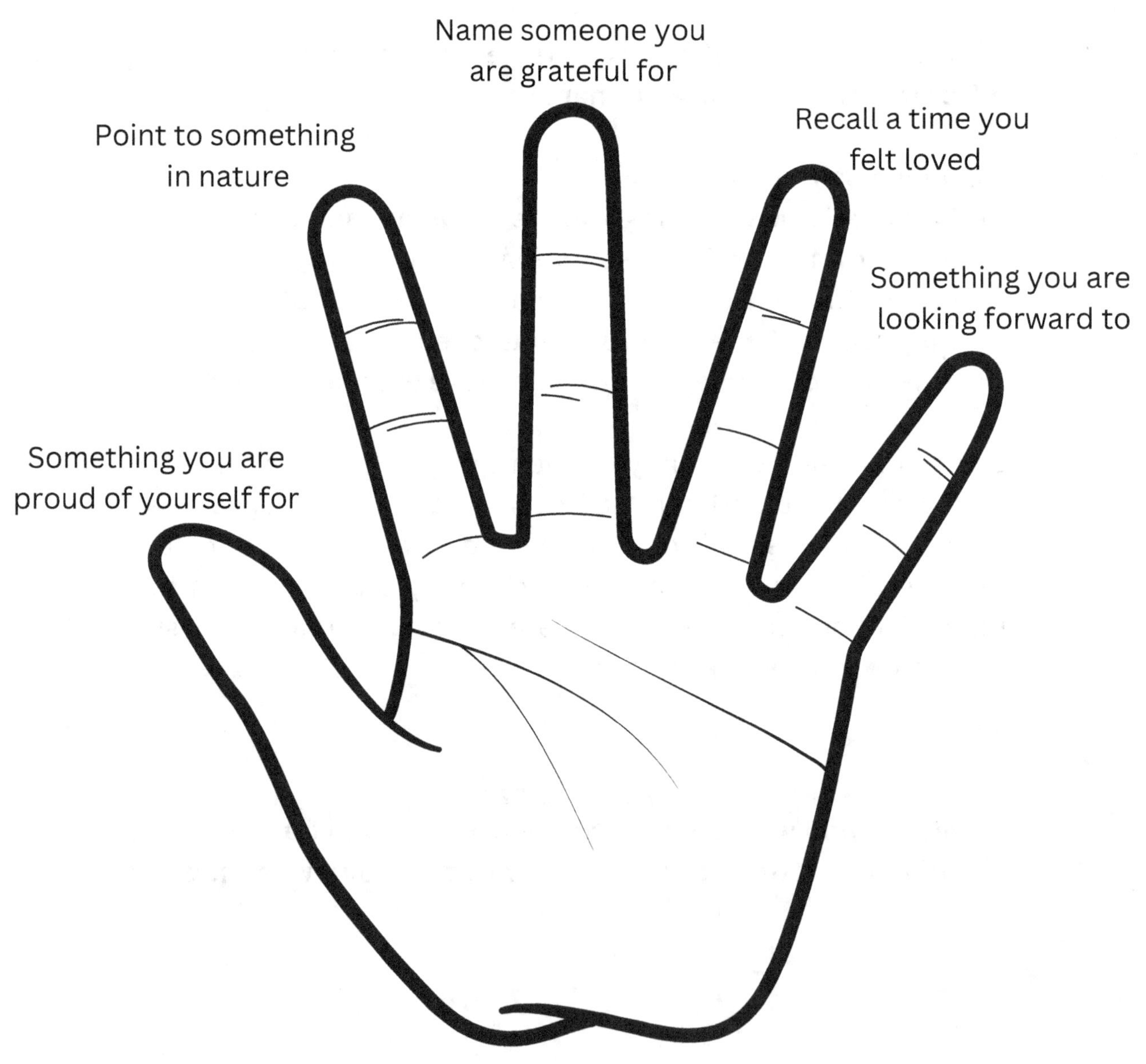

WEEKLY

REVIEW

PROS OF THIS WEEK'S SKILL

____

____

____

CONS OF THIS WEEK'S SKILL

____

____

____

WOO – HOO OF THE WEEK

____

____

____

____

REACTIONS TO THIS WEEK'S SKILL

____

____

____

____

____

____

____

____

____

DIFFICULTY OF SKILL

(1) (2) (3) (4) (5) (6) (7)

USEFULNESS OF SKILL

(1) (2) (3) (4) (5) (6) (7)

OVERALL MOOD THIS WEEK

NOTES

____

____

FEEL YOUR FEELINGS

EMOTIONAL REGULATION SKILLS

"I FEEL BECAUSE" JOURNALING ACTIVITY

"I feel because" is a great way to acknowledge and validate your emotions.

"I feel because" can be used at any time even as a random check-in with yourself.

Take the pen to paper and just go until you physically cannot connect to anymore feelings. Don't be afraid to repeat feelings. You may experience three feelings towards one "because" and that's fine too. Just write them as separate "I feel because" statements.

Try this one out a couple of times. Even if you can only connect to three feelings it's a great start.

If you are new to connecting to feelings and identifying them, then focus on just the process of identifying and labeling feelings. A great tool to help you with this is a feeling wheel. (You can find examples online.)

Benefits:
- *Provides you with the opportunity to own your feelings.*
- *Feel emotions in a controlled and validating manner.*
- *Stating the event, thought, or experience that triggered the feeling helps validate the feeling.*

"I FEEL BECAUSE" JOURNALING ACTIVITY

"I Feel ____Because . . . " Example:
- **I feel ashamed because my boss was upset with me when I was late to work today.**
- **I feel embarrassed because when my boss asked me why I was late, I couldn't explain that my bus was caught in traffic.**
- **I feel worried because I think my boss thinks I am irresponsible.**

A couple of things to look at in these statements. Feelings are never wrong! Feelings are just feelings. They can always change!

The shame in this example is a direct result of being reprimanded by the boss for being late. Is there anything that can be changed in this example? Yes! Work on being on time or early. However, after reading more into the journal entry you will see that the individual was late because the bus was caught in traffic. So, this was out of his/her control, and it is a moment of accepting the reality as it is.

This is an example of how journaling in this way allows you to further process your emotions and thoughts!

I FEEL BECAUSE JOURNALING ACTIVITY

I FEEL ____ BECAUSE . . .

WEEKLY

REVIEW

PROS OF THIS WEEK'S SKILL

____

____

____

CONS OF THIS WEEK'S SKILL

____

____

____

WOO – HOO OF THE WEEK

____

____

____

____

REACTIONS TO THIS WEEK'S SKILL

____

____

____

____

____

____

____

____

DIFFICULTY OF SKILL

(1) (2) (3) (4) (5) (6) (7)

USEFULNESS OF SKILL

(1) (2) (3) (4) (5) (6) (7)

OVERALL MOOD THIS WEEK

NOTES

____

BODY SCAN MEDITATION

This week's technique is a form of meditation which directly helps in the mind-body connection. You will be practicing the body scan meditation.

Body scans encourage you to focus intently on one area of your body at a time noticing any tension, pain, tightness, or other sensations. The key component of noticing these sensations is to learn to do so without judgement. Focus on just noticing the sensations, not tying any meaning to the sensation that you feel and moving along to the next part of the body.

How does one do a body scan? Included in the appendix (page 182) is a script for a body-scan you can record yourself or have someone do it for you. **Or if you'd like head over to our YouTube Channel at www.youtube.com/@LetGoLetBe.**

You can also find videos and apps online, so definitely try a few out. In the beginning start with a 7-10-minute-long scan and slowly build up in time. Once you get the hang of body scans, they can be performed in your head when needed.

Body scans have shown to help in reducing anxiety, improving relaxation and sleep, and assisting in pain management. With an on-going meditation practice one can see an improvement in concentration, redirection of self, and self-awareness.

If you have trouble sleeping, try this skill before bed. I dare you too, you probably won't get past your shoulders! And those nervous flyers out there – a body scan is a great tool during take-off.

BODY SCAN MEDITATION

Benefits:
- *Learn how your emotions influence physical sensations.*
- *Allows sensations to flow naturally without holding on to a prescribed meaning or feeling.*
- *Activates the parasympathetic nervous system which in turn helps relax the "fight or flight" response.*
- *Increases awareness of stress related symptoms to help you better manage stress in the future.*
- *Reduces racing or intrusive thoughts while performing meditation and managing these thoughts outside of meditation.*
- *Teaches the art of being present in one's body and remaining in the here and now.*
- *Teaches a nonjudgmental approach to being with oneself, which has shown to assist in reducing physical pain for some.*

QUICK TIP
Let's get one thing straight.
"Meditation does not have to look any type of way!"
Even 2-3 minutes can help improve your mood.

REVIEW

PROS OF THIS WEEK'S SKILL

____

____

____

CONS OF THIS WEEK'S SKILL

____

____

____

WOO – HOO OF THE WEEK

____

____

____

____

REACTIONS TO THIS WEEK'S SKILL

____

____

____

____

____

____

____

____

DIFFICULTY OF SKILL

(1) (2) (3) (4) (5) (6) (7)

USEFULNESS OF SKILL

(1) (2) (3) (4) (5) (6) (7)

OVERALL MOOD THIS WEEK

NOTES

____

____

SIT WITH IT

This week when a feeling starts to overcome you sit down and use the FEAR technique. This week's skill is based on distress tolerance and learning to sit in discomfort.

FEAR in this case stands for FEELING, EXPERIENCE, ATTEND, and RELEASE. This technique will assist you in feeling your feelings, allowing yourself to experience the emotions, attending to these feelings and your needs, and then releasing the feelings.

How does this work?

- Feeling: Once you have sat down ask yourself what emotions am I feeling? Use those "I feel . . . because" statements. Say it out loud!
- Experience: Allow the physical reactions to come that are triggered by your feelings. Tears, rapid heart rate, or an inability to sit with it.
- Attend: Take a deep breath and return to "I feel. . .because" then remind yourself this feeling will pass. "I have the ability to feel it and let it go." You may have to mindfully repeat this to yourself several times. You may need to encourage yourself to remain in the discomfort. Ask yourself if there is anything you physically need to help yourself in this moment? Maybe you just need time. Maybe you need to hold something such as a worry stone or a soft blanket.
- Release: This is the moment when the emotion begins to lessen. You may be using your breath to help release the intensity of the emotion. You might have to use self-talk to remind yourself that the situation will not impact you in two weeks, two days, or even two hours from now. Help release the discomfort until you start to physically feel lighter and more comfortable sitting with yourself again.

SIT WITH IT

Breaking the habit of avoidance and denial can be threatening and overwhelming at first. You may fear experiencing your feelings due to a history of being highjacked by them. But now you have developed skills to help you become more comfortable with the discomfort associated with your feelings. You have learned how to calm yourself and control your feelings.

Benefits:
- *Increases distress tolerance and self-soothing skills.*
- *Increases acceptance and self-love.*
- *Helps develop emotional regulation skills.*

WEEKLY

REVIEW

PROS OF THIS WEEK'S SKILL

____

____

____

CONS OF THIS WEEK'S SKILL

____

____

____

WOO – HOO OF THE WEEK

____

____

____

____

REACTIONS TO THIS WEEK'S SKILL

____

____

____

____

____

____

____

DIFFICULTY OF SKILL

① ② ③ ④ ⑤ ⑥ ⑦

USEFULNESS OF SKILL

① ② ③ ④ ⑤ ⑥ ⑦

OVERALL MOOD THIS WEEK

😊 🙂 😮 😠 😟 😎 😐

NOTES

____

____

WHAT IS YOUR BODY TELLING YOU?

This week you will be performing a meditation practice to re-connect to your body so you will be more in tune with interpreting the sensations you experience after you've completed the meditation. <u>Follow the guided meditation included in the appendix on page 187</u> or you can find a recording of this meditation on our YouTube Channel at <u>www.youtube.com/@LetGoLetBe.</u>

In a previous week you participated in a body scan as a method of learning meditation and increasing your mindfulness. This week's skill will be connecting with your body to understand the manifestation of your emotions within your physical self.

Benefits:

- *Gain awareness of early warning signs of distressing emotions and identify them faster. Reduces physical symptoms of anxiety or anger faster and more efficiently.*
- *Ability to identify patterns related to the mind-body connection.*
- *Increases confidence in your ability to manage emotions and avoid acting out behaviors.*

What Does your Body Say Example:
My jaw is one of the first things to become tense. I use this as a sign to check-in with my stress. Another discovery was the narrowing of my shoulders and closing off my chest when feeling insecure or inadequate. I now consciously will roll my shoulders back and lift my chest up which improves not only my posture but my mood too!

WHAT'S YOUR BODY TELLING YOU?

JOURNAL HERE

REVIEW

PROS OF THIS WEEK'S SKILL

____

____

____

CONS OF THIS WEEK'S SKILL

____

____

____

WOO – HOO OF THE WEEK

____

____

____

____

REACTIONS TO THIS WEEK'S SKILL

____

____

____

____

____

____

____

____

DIFFICULTY OF SKILL

(1) (2) (3) (4) (5) (6) (7)

USEFULNESS OF SKILL

(1) (2) (3) (4) (5) (6) (7)

OVERALL MOOD THIS WEEK

NOTES

____

EARLY WARNING SIGNS

This week is about identifying your early warning signs to a potentially more upsetting moment. Follow the worksheet included to explore your physical, emotional, and behavioral reactions are to stress and anxiety.

- **List the ways stress or anxiety shows up for you physically, emotionally, and behaviorally.**
- **Circle 3-4 of these early warning signs you find the most challenging to cope with.**
- **Brainstorm 2 possible methods to alleviate that specific early warning sign.**

Learning to identify these signs can help in maintaining a stable mood for the future. By knowing how you react to the buildup of stress or anxiety you can implement skills prior to feeling overwhelmed or experiencing panic like symptoms.

Benefits:
- *Feel more empowered.*
- *Increases control over behaviors and reactions to stress, anxiety, and anger.*
- *Decreases irritability and promotes mindfulness.*

EARLY WARNING SIGNS

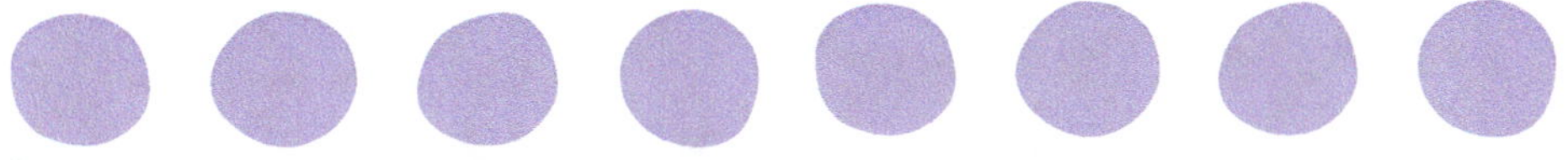

PHYSICAL SIGNS

Palms start to sweat.
Jaw clenches.
Headache behind my eyes.

EMOTIONAL SIGNS

Easily annoyed by things and people.
Feel overwhelmed by others.

BEHAVIORAL SIGNS

Brain feels like it's going a mile a minute with racing thoughts.
Doing multiple tasks at once but accomplish little.

EARLY WARNING SIGNS

EARLY WARNING SIGNS

SIGN OF STRESS OR ANXIETY

WHAT TO DO TO HELP YOURSELF?

Easily annoyed by things and people.

Brain feels like it's going a mile a minute with racing thoughts.

Take alone time on purpose for myself. Set boundaries for myself and others.

PAUSE - sit quietly and do 4 Square Breathing.

REVIEW

PROS OF THIS WEEK'S SKILL

____

____

____

CONS OF THIS WEEK'S SKILL

____

____

____

WOO – HOO OF THE WEEK

____

____

____

____

REACTIONS TO THIS WEEK'S SKILL

____

____

____

____

____

____

____

____

DIFFICULTY OF SKILL

(1) (2) (3) (4) (5) (6) (7)

USEFULNESS OF SKILL

(1) (2) (3) (4) (5) (6) (7)

OVERALL MOOD THIS WEEK

NOTES

____

UNDERSTANDING ANGER

This week you will be using the accompanied worksheet to help uncover some of the primary emotions that lie beneath any anger you are experiencing.

This skill can help in uncovering feelings from the past that could be contributing to feelings of resentment currently. Or the worksheets can be used in a more immediate situation when you experience anger in the present day.

If you get nothing else from this week's skill hold onto the knowledge that anger is a SECONDARY EMOTION!

What does that mean? It means that often anger is in response to another emotion or several other emotions. You're cut off while driving down the highway, you get angry right? Yes, but why are you angry? Perhaps the person that cut you off almost caused an accident which means you felt scared or threatened.

Another example, a friend confronts you about something you did or said that concerns them, but you respond with anger. Ask yourself do I feel anything else in response to this? You may discover you feel embarrassed, ashamed, or hurt by their comment.

Tips to Uncovering the Primary Emotions:
- *Think about the last time you felt angry for a moment and dig slightly deeper into your response.*
- *What was the initial stimuli or event that prompted you to feel angry?*
- *Ask yourself what other emotions did I feel at the time?*
- *Remember you can refer to a feeling wheel to help identify feelings. You used this tool during Feel Your Feelings, Skill 1 on page 22.*

UNDERSTANDING ANGER

<u>Don't get me wrong anger is a legit feeling!</u>
<u>It is not right nor wrong to feel angry!</u>

Some of the most iconic changes happened because someone was angry. Without being angry we would not confront problems and look for resolutions or change. But it is important to recognize that beneath that anger lies feelings of hurt, betrayal, disgust, injustice, and many other possible emotions.

Benefits:
- *Identifying primary emotions promotes healing and letting go of unhelpful behavioral patterns.*
- *Feeling all your emotions leads to gaining self-control of feelings, thoughts, and reactions.*
- *A higher level of self-awareness increases self-confidence.*
- *Managing anger more effectively aids in better communication and emotional regulation (fancy talk for managing your feelings).*

UNDERSTANDING ANGER

YOU GOT TO FEEL IT TO HEAL IT!

WHAT IS IT THAT I AM ANGRY ABOUT?

____

____

____

____

WHEN I THINK ABOUT THIS WHAT DOES MY INTERNAL MONOLUGE SAY?

____

____

____

____

UNDERSTANDING ANGER

YOU GOT TO FEEL IT TO HEAL IT!

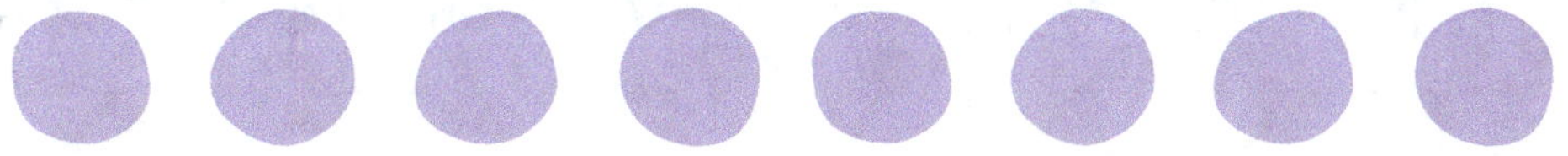

HOW DOES WHAT I AM SAYING ABOUT THE SITUATION MAKE ME FEEL?

ARE THESE FEELINGS UNCOMFORTABLE? IF SO EXPLAIN WHAT MAKES THEM UNCOMFORTABLE.

AND NOW ALLOW YOURSELF TO FEEL ALL OF THESE FEELINGS BY REPEATING
"I AM ANGRY BECAUSE I DO NOT LIKE FEELING _____."

WEEKLY

REVIEW

PROS OF THIS WEEK'S SKILL

____

____

____

CONS OF THIS WEEK'S SKILL

____

____

____

WOO – HOO OF THE WEEK

____

____

____

____

REACTIONS TO THIS WEEK'S SKILL

____

____

____

____

____

____

____

____

DIFFICULTY OF SKILL

① ② ③ ④ ⑤ ⑥ ⑦

USEFULNESS OF SKILL

① ② ③ ④ ⑤ ⑥ ⑦

OVERALL MOOD THIS WEEK

NOTES

____

____

FIND YOUR WISE MIND

This week you will be using the included worksheet to help discover what Dialectical Behavior Therapy calls the Wise Mind. You will create a dialogue between the Rational Mind and the Emotional Mind.

- **First select a situation from this week that upset you.**
- **Ask yourself what each state of your mind says about this situation. Allow yourself to brain storm from each perceptive.**
- **One side represents the Rational Mind, and the other side represents the Emotional Mind. The overlap of the two circles of the Venn diagram represents the Wise Mind.**
- **After exploring the Rational and Emotional Mind you will then approach the situation from a Wise Mind place.**

The *Emotional* and *Rational Mind* theory comes from Dialectical Behavior Therapy. The concept discusses how your mind has three states the *Rational Mind*, the *Emotional Mind*, and the *Wise Mind*. This week's skill can seem complicated but once you get the hang of how these states of your mind think it will make more sense.

Let's start with *The Rational Mind:*
- Thinks from a logical place.
- Focus is on facts and actual events that took place.
- Is analytical and does not have much concern for emotions.
- May intellectualize situations or feelings.
- Will approach situations with a plan.
- Decision making based on logic and facts. While this is not always a bad thing there are times in which it is important to consider one's emotional reaction before proceeding in decision making.

FIND YOUR WISE MIND

On the other hand, *The Emotional Mind* is much more irrational, sometimes even impulsive in nature.

The Emotional Mind:
- Behaviors that are a direct reaction from an emotional state.
- May react impulsively without considering the consequences of their behavior.
- Feelings control thoughts and behaviors which can lead to feelings of guilt or shame.

The Wise Mind
- A balance between the *Rational* and *Emotional Minds*.
- Acknowledges and validates your feelings.
- Approaches feelings with respect and reason.
- Allows you to respond to feelings with respect for yourself and others.

The goal to this exercise is to utilize the knowledge of The Rational Mind and The Emotional Mind to unlock the power of The Wise Mind.

Remember:
YOU HAVE TO FEEL IT TO HEAL IT!

FIND YOUR WISE MIND

Managing the feelings to navigate your behaviors and responses will empower you to making rational and effective decisions.

Benefits:
- *Improves emotional regulation skills.*
- *Reduces sabotaging behaviors.*
- *Aids in mind-body connectivity.*
- *Empowers the individual.*
- *Reduces impulsive behaviors.*

<u>Find Your Wise Mind Example:</u>
- **On the following page you will find an example of an individual having an open discussion with the Rational and Emotional Mind about their boyfriend not responding right away to a text message.**
- **Notice the statements the Emotional Mind makes. These statements demonstrate Catastrophic Thinking Patterns and Fortune-Telling or Jumping to Conclusions.**
- **Notice the Rational Mind using logic to hypothesize why he is not responding.**
- **Take notice of the integration that happens in the Wise Mind for the person to calm down and accept the situation.**

FIND YOUR WISE MIND

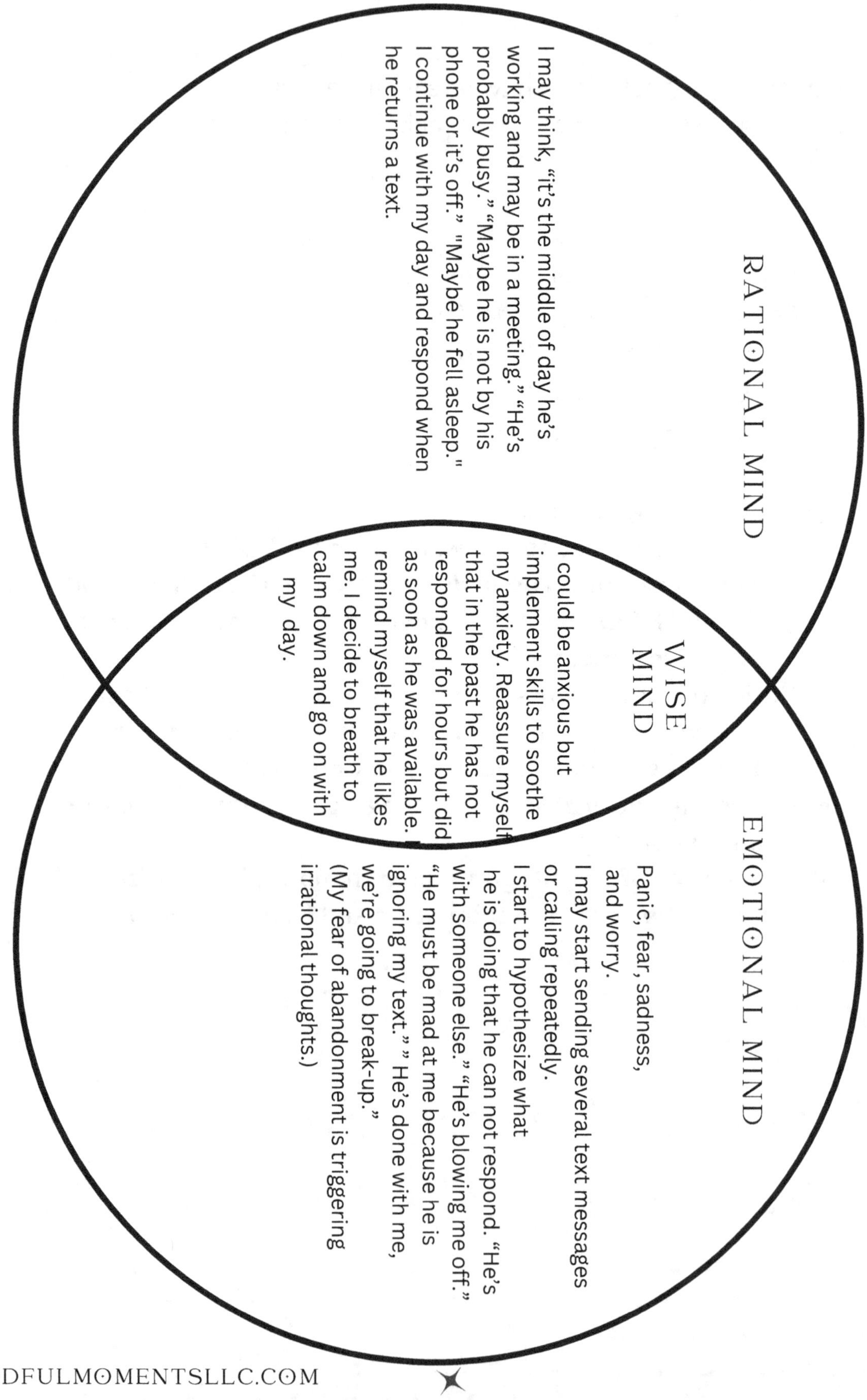

RATIONAL MIND

I may think, "it's the middle of day he's working and may be in a meeting." "He's probably busy." "Maybe he is not by his phone or it's off." "Maybe he fell asleep." I continue with my day and respond when he returns a text.

WISE MIND

I could be anxious but implement skills to soothe my anxiety. Reassure myself that in the past he has not responded for hours but did as soon as he was available. I remind myself that he likes me. I decide to breath to calm down and go on with my day.

EMOTIONAL MIND

Panic, fear, sadness, and worry.
I may start sending several text messages or calling repeatedly.
I start to hypothesize what he is doing that he can not respond. "He's with someone else." "He's blowing me off." "He must be mad at me because he is ignoring my text." " He's done with me, we're going to break-up."
(My fear of abandonment is triggering irrational thoughts.)

FIND YOUR WISE MIND

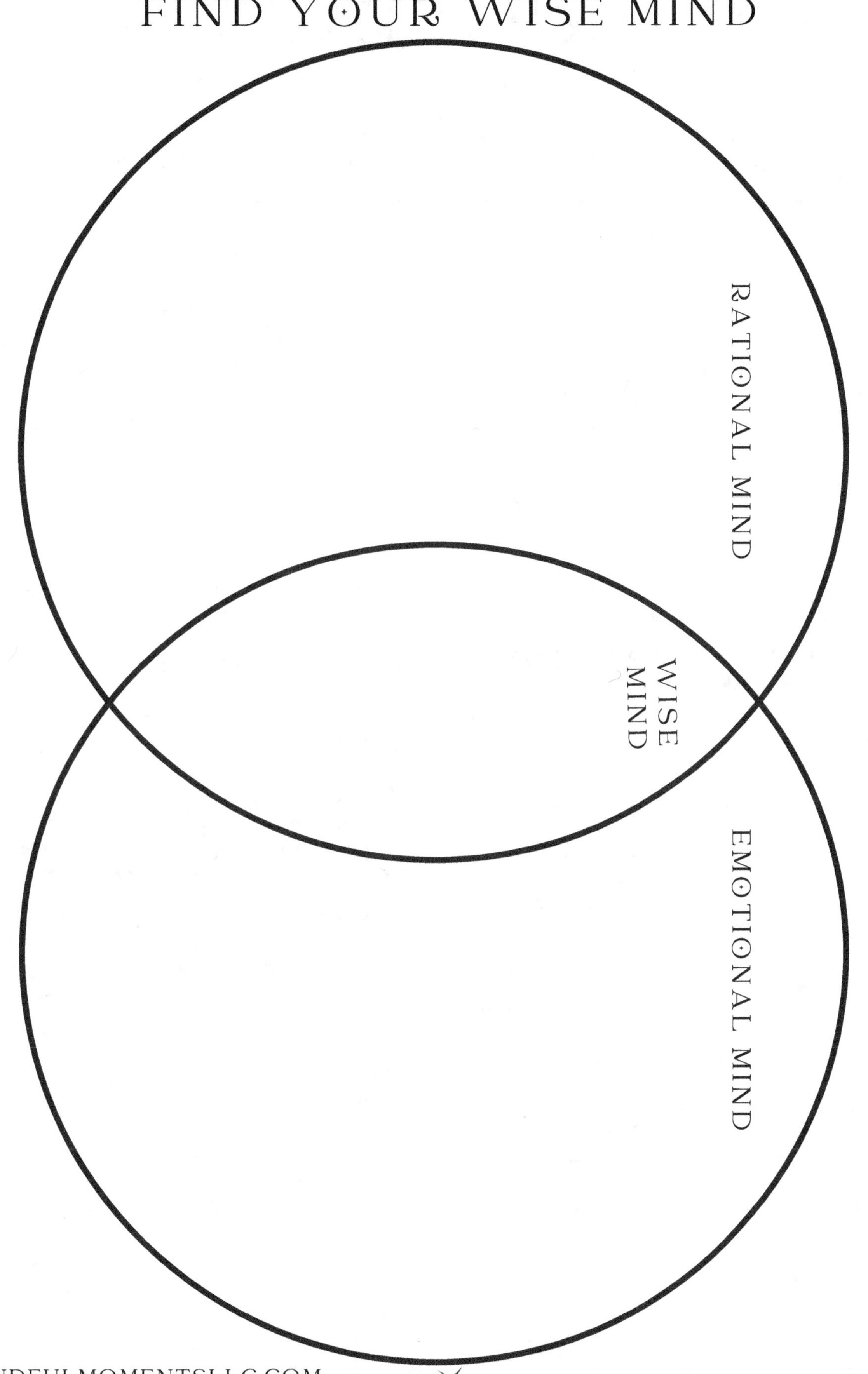

REVIEW

PROS OF THIS WEEK'S SKILL

____

____

____

CONS OF THIS WEEK'S SKILL

____

____

____

WOO – HOO OF THE WEEK

____

____

____

____

REACTIONS TO THIS WEEK'S SKILL

____

____

____

____

____

____

____

____

____

DIFFICULTY OF SKILL

(1) (2) (3) (4) (5) (6) (7)

USEFULNESS OF SKILL

(1) (2) (3) (4) (5) (6) (7)

OVERALL MOOD THIS WEEK

NOTES

____

BE POSITIVE

ENCOURAGEMENT SKILLS

DAILY GRINDS & GRATITUDE

This week you will be practicing gratitude by creating a gratitude list.

To start practicing gratitude, begin with just 3 things you are grateful for. This small practice can go a very long way in setting the tone of your day.

A fun way to integrate this into your life is making it a part of your morning ritual. Perhaps while sipping your coffee (get it grinds and gratitude, coffee grinds) you can easily keep a small notepad by you and just add 3 things each morning.

This list does not have to be extravagant. Often, we forget the importance of ordinary.

Try this out three days this week and see how it impacts your thinking. Even if it improves your mood just 10% on one of those days. Then imagine if you used this more often what it could do for you.

Benefits:
- *Reduces stress, worry, and anxiety.*
- *Improves the practice of positive thinking.*
- *Helps strengthen neuron pathways through neuroplasticity.*
- *Creates healthier and happier thought patterns and feelings.*

DAILY GRINDS & GRATITUDE

GRATITUDE LIST

- I am grateful for having the opportunity to peacefully drink a hot cup of coffee this morning.

- I am grateful to live in my home.

- I am grateful to have been able to talk with a friend from college on the phone last night.

- I am grateful for my coping skills.

GRATITUDE LIST

REVIEW

PROS OF THIS WEEK'S SKILL

____

____

____

CONS OF THIS WEEK'S SKILL

____

____

____

WOO – HOO OF THE WEEK

____

____

____

____

REACTIONS TO THIS WEEK'S SKILL

____

____

____

____

____

____

____

____

DIFFICULTY OF SKILL

1 2 3 4 5 6 7

USEFULNESS OF SKILL

1 2 3 4 5 6 7

OVERALL MOOD THIS WEEK

NOTES

____

____

TADA LIST

Try out your own Tada List a few times throughout the week and notice if you see a difference in the way you view your daily tasks and chores.

The Tada List is like thought reframing but for your to-do list. The concept behind the Tada List is to write down each thing you complete for the day.

Ever notice how anxiety provoking a to-do list can be? If you are the type that tends to continuously add to your to-do list, there comes a point in which it feels defeating and never-ending. You start to think you have accomplished nothing.

The Tada List allows you to see the facts and the tasks you have completed. By seeing this evidence, it makes it easier to leave those negative statements about yourself behind.

The Tada List is a great alternative!

Benefits:
- *Creates a sense of accomplishment.*
- *Increases self-validation and self-esteem.*
- *Increases motivation and productivity.*

TADA LIST

TADA

- Folded and put laundry away.
- Called and made eye doctor appointment.
- Finished project at work before deadline.
- Worked out for 30 minutes.

TADA

-
-
-
-

REVIEW

PROS OF THIS WEEK'S SKILL

____

____

____

CONS OF THIS WEEK'S SKILL

____

____

____

WOO – HOO OF THE WEEK

____

____

____

____

REACTIONS TO THIS WEEK'S SKILL

____

____

____

____

____

____

____

____

DIFFICULTY OF SKILL

① ② ③ ④ ⑤ ⑥ ⑦

USEFULNESS OF SKILL

① ② ③ ④ ⑤ ⑥ ⑦

OVERALL MOOD THIS WEEK

NOTES

____

____

AFFIRMATIONS

For this week choose one affirmation to practice daily. Affirmations are a form of positive self-talk which activate the reward center of your brain and the area involved in self-processing.

- **To get started ask yourself, what do I really wish I believed about myself? Or ask what is something I often tell myself that I know is not helpful? You can then take that statement and reframe the unhelpful thought, see Change Your Thoughts, Skill 1 on page 71 for more on reframing a thought.**

- **Affirmations start to integrate into your sense of being as you repeat them. You may even start to perform in alignment with them.**

- **Repetition is required. So, flood your brain waves with affirmations. Leave a sticky note on your bathroom mirror so you can see it in the morning and the evening. Set it as a reminder on your phone for when you wake up in the morning or at lunch time. Download an affirmation app or purchase a daily affirmation book for your nightstand.**

Like most things it is about practice, if you have spent years telling yourself "I can't," guess what, most likely you won't. But if you change that statement to "I can," you will start to do the thing you once believed you could not do.

AFFIRMATIONS

Benefits:
- *Increases self-awareness and self-esteem.*
- *Aids in neuroplasticity which rewires the brain and the messages it sends.*
- *Increases positive thinking patterns and improves mindset about yourself and your world.*

Affirmations Example:
I spent most of my earlier years telling myself I could not run because growing up I was diagnosed with Osgood-Schlatter disease. I didn't know what it was.

In my twenties I hired a trainer to help me learn to run. Long story short, he taught me everything I needed to know; how to land on my feet, how to pace, how to breath. But what my trainer didn't know was the story running through my head for the better part of two decades. "I can't run, I have bad knees." With every attempt my knees would hurt, and I would return to walking instead. Until I decided to apply my own methods to my self-sabotaging thoughts.

I started to focus on the thought "I can run" and paced myself for short intervals to see that I could run for 2 minutes straight with no pain. I built up from there and eventually the gal who could not run, became a runner, and ran several half marathons. Best of all without any knee pain!

AFFIRMATIONS

WHAT ARE YOUR AFFIRMATIONS?

REVIEW

PROS OF THIS WEEK'S SKILL

____

____

____

CONS OF THIS WEEK'S SKILL

____

____

____

WOO – HOO OF THE WEEK

____

____

____

____

REACTIONS TO THIS WEEK'S SKILL

____

____

____

____

____

____

____

DIFFICULTY OF SKILL

1 2 3 4 5 6 7

USEFULNESS OF SKILL

1 2 3 4 5 6 7

OVERALL MOOD THIS WEEK

NOTES

____

____

FLIP IT TO THE POSITIVE

Flipping a thought or reframing the thought is a two-step skill.

The first step is to catch the negative thought and the second is to then flip it to a positive. This week find at least three negative thoughts and attempt to reframe them for yourself.

Now, you may say, "yeah but I don't believe the positive." It is very likely you do not believe the thought due to years of practicing negative self-talk. That's okay for now the skill is about rewiring your thinking pattern. By reframing to the positive the neurological pathways which carry positive thinking can strengthen. Therefore, the more practice the better!

Strategies to flip the thought include thinking the opposite or challenging the thought's accuracy by asking how true the statement is. A personal favorite of mine for reframing is when you catch yourself using negative self-talk. Ask yourself would I say this to my friend? If the answer is no, then it is time to reframe the thought.

Reframing is a highly useful and effective tool and a great skill to learn to incorporate daily.

Before you know it you will be catching and changing thoughts on the regular!

FLIP IT TO THE POSITIVE

FLIP IT TO THE POSITIVE

- I'm never going to get that promotion – In time I will get that promotion or find an even better opportunity.

- I worry all the time – I can adapt and go with the flow.

- I'm a mess – I am human.

- I can't do this – I can do many things.

FLIP IT TO THE POSITIVE

REVIEW

PROS OF THIS WEEK'S SKILL

CONS OF THIS WEEK'S SKILL

WOO – HOO OF THE WEEK

REACTIONS TO THIS WEEK'S SKILL

DIFFICULTY OF SKILL

① ② ③ ④ ⑤ ⑥ ⑦

USEFULNESS OF SKILL

① ② ③ ④ ⑤ ⑥ ⑦

OVERALL MOOD THIS WEEK

NOTES

CHART IT OUT

This week you will use a pie chart to help map out how you are utilizing your time.

Have you ever felt like there isn't enough time in your day? Or that you just didn't seem to get enough done? Ever look back at your day and wonder how it took you so long to get your errands done for the day? How about telling others I don't have time for self-care?

Start with the basics: brushing your teeth, making breakfast, walking the dog, getting dressed and ready for work. Divide your pie chart up into increments of time that you find yourself using on your activities throughout the day. Reflect on this chart at the end of the day and allow it to help you manage your time to your liking for the days to come.

Some days you may feel extremely proud and accomplished. Other days you may find you could use more time to fit in R&R for yourself. The pie chart is another great method of helping you develop a sense of work-life balance on a more regular basis.

Benefits:
- *Increases insight into your daily living activities.*
- *Helps understand your use of time management and improve on it.*
- *Validates how much you do accomplish in a day.*
- *Combats negative self-talk and self-doubt with evidence of your ability to accomplish tasks.*
- *Improves a sense of harmony between your work and personal life.*

CHART IT OUT

Chart It Out Example:

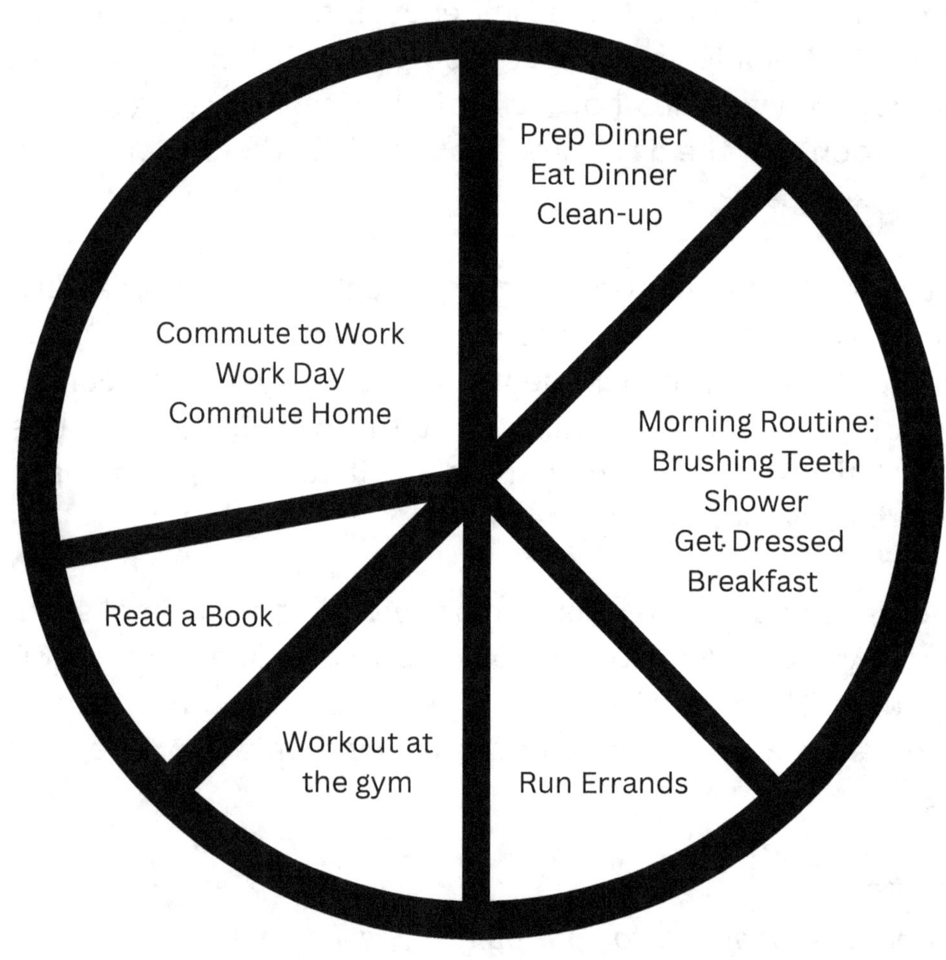

CHART IT OUT

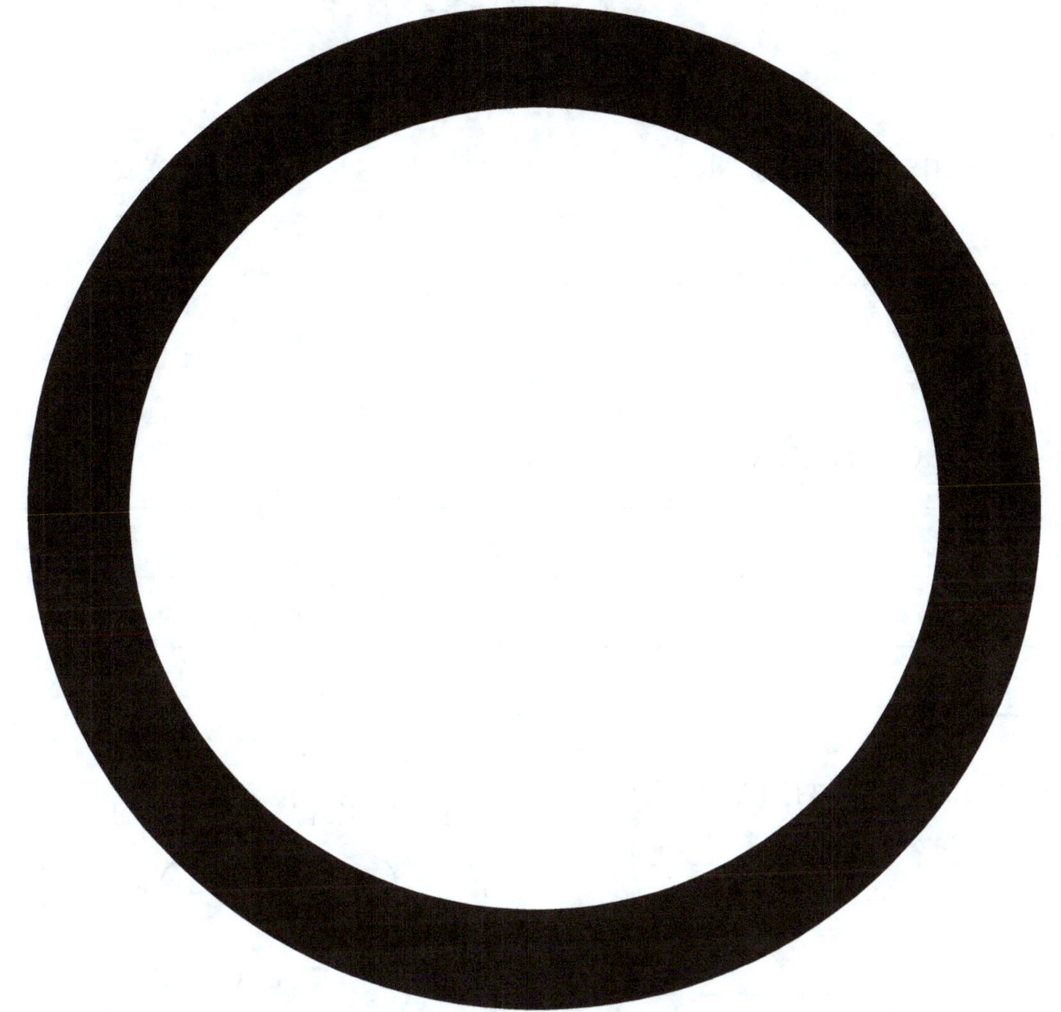

MY ACTIVITIES

REVIEW

PROS OF THIS WEEK'S SKILL

____

____

____

CONS OF THIS WEEK'S SKILL

____

____

____

WOO – HOO OF THE WEEK

____

____

____

____

REACTIONS TO THIS WEEK'S SKILL

____

____

____

____

____

____

____

DIFFICULTY OF SKILL

(1) (2) (3) (4) (5) (6) (7)

USEFULNESS OF SKILL

(1) (2) (3) (4) (5) (6) (7)

OVERALL MOOD THIS WEEK

NOTES

____

SUPRISE GREETING CARDS

A fun activity to do for yourself is to buy a few greeting cards from the dollar store and write out a thoughtful or encouraging card to yourself. For this week's skill you will be writing your future-self greeting cards for a little future woo-hoo or pick-me up.

- **Grab a "just thinking of you" card or two and maybe a "congratulations" card.**
- **Take some time this week and write out a thoughtful message to your future self.**
- **Address and stamp the envelopes.**
- **Ask a trusted friend or family member if they would hold on to the cards and periodically mail one out to you.**

The fun of this is you never know when the card will show up in your mailbox. And hopefully this trusted individual will know just about when you could use some self-praise and encouragement. Try to have some fun with this one. It's a skill that's meant to be lighthearted!

Benefits:
- *Encourages and strengthens positive self-talk.*
- *Improves self-validation.*
- *Aids in developing positive affirmations.*
- *Enhances self-esteem and self-worth.*

<u>QUICK TIP:</u>
You may have to come back later to the weekly review for this skill after you get your first card in the mail. Or you can review what you think of the idea and how difficult it was or wasn't to write a card out to yourself.

WEEKLY

REVIEW

PROS OF THIS WEEK'S SKILL

____

____

____

CONS OF THIS WEEK'S SKILL

____

____

____

WOO – HOO OF THE WEEK

____

____

____

____

REACTIONS TO THIS WEEK'S SKILL

____

____

____

____

____

____

____

____

DIFFICULTY OF SKILL

(1) (2) (3) (4) (5) (6) (7)

USEFULNESS OF SKILL

(1) (2) (3) (4) (5) (6) (7)

OVERALL MOOD THIS WEEK

NOTES

____

THE GRATITUDE JAR

This week goes back to the use of gratitude. You will be making a gratitude jar.

- **Use an old jar or purchase a new one to create a Gratitude Jar. Feel free to decorate this jar as you wish or find fun pens and slips of paper to help make the jar more attractive to you.**
- **Write something or someone you are grateful for, fold the paper and place it into the jar. After some time, your jar will be filled with tons of gratitude and appreciation.**
- **When feeling down you can open your jar and read through all the wonderful things you have in your world.**

This activity is also a great family tool. Keep the jar in the living room or dining room and get everyone involved in it. After some time, you may find that your gratitude grows and comes more naturally which also means your mindset will most likely be in a more positive place.

Keeping a mindset focused on positivity and gratitude is a healing mindset.

REVIEW

PROS OF THIS WEEK'S SKILL

CONS OF THIS WEEK'S SKILL

WOO – HOO OF THE WEEK

REACTIONS TO THIS WEEK'S SKILL

DIFFICULTY OF SKILL

1 2 3 4 5 6 7

USEFULNESS OF SKILL

1 2 3 4 5 6 7

OVERALL MOOD THIS WEEK

NOTES

CHANGE YOUR THOUGHTS

COGNITIVE TECHNIQUES & COGNITIVE BEHAVIORAL SKILLS

END STINKING THINKING

Using this week's skill, you will learn to identify irrational thoughts, challenge these thoughts, and restructure the thought to be more accurate and helpful to you.

STEPS TO CHANGE STINKING THINKING
- Ask yourself how true is this thought? 0 (totally false) – 100 (totally true)
- Then assess if this thought is any of those unhelpful thoughts? (See Appendix for Stinking Thinking worksheet, page 188)
  - If yes, well guess what? It can't be 100% true then!
- What actual evidence or facts do you have to prove or disprove your thought to be true? Identify for both sides.
- After finding evidence, review it. Now ask yourself based on the evidence how true is the thought, 0 – 100?
- If the number is less than when you started, it's time to create a more accurate thought based on your facts and evidence. If the number is the same, ask yourself what can I control or change that will help the situation or myself?

QUICK TIP:
Use a PEN & PAPER to do this. It will be easier to navigate that way.

This skill can be challenging but with practice over this next week you will find yourself identifying irrational or unhelpful thought patterns that impact your mood and behaviors. Learning to understand the dynamics between your feelings, thoughts, and behaviors can be one of your most powerful tools.

END STINKING THINKING

Stinking thinking is formally known as cognitive distortions, which simply put is distorted thinking patterns. What does this mean? It means that the thoughts you are having about a particular person, thing, event, or even an emotion are not 100% accurate.

Inaccurate thinking patterns can lead to misinterpreting your experiences and creates upsetting emotions. During these times of distress, you may find yourself reacting rather than responding to your feelings and your behaviors. Reacting behaviors may include angry outbursts, impulsive behaviors, or uncontrollable crying spells.

Benefits:
- *Realistic and accurate thinking improves mood, self-esteem, and self-confidence.*
- *Helpful thinking patterns creates rational behaviors and responses to feelings, events, and situations.*
- *Improves ability in managing upsetting events, relationships, and emotions overall.*

WEEKLY

REVIEW

PROS OF THIS WEEK'S SKILL

____

____

____

CONS OF THIS WEEK'S SKILL

____

____

____

WOO – HOO OF THE WEEK

____

____

____

____

REACTIONS TO THIS WEEK'S SKILL

____

____

____

____

____

____

____

____

DIFFICULTY OF SKILL

① ② ③ ④ ⑤ ⑥ ⑦

USEFULNESS OF SKILL

① ② ③ ④ ⑤ ⑥ ⑦

OVERALL MOOD THIS WEEK

NOTES

____

____

3–MINUTE CATASTROPHE

This week's skill is almost like getting to play a game, take 3-minutes to think of the worst-case scenario when you feel overwhelmed or worried by something and intentionally rant until you reach your worst nightmare about the situation.

- **Set a timer for 3-minutes.**
- **Begin speaking out loud to yourself or a trusted friend or family member just how bad this thing is.**
- **Do not hold back. Purposely allow your mind to go extreme and say the most outlandish and absurd things that come to mind.**
- **When 3-minutes are up you are done going down that road.**
- **Now ask yourself "Okay, what's more likely to happen?" I bet it's not nearly as anxiety provoking.**

People can make a mountain out of a molehill with catastrophizing thoughts. This can happen naturally as when one's brain becomes hard-wired to think in this manner it becomes almost a default setting. It is easy to be unaware of how often or frequent this occurs in your day-to-day life. When executing the skill with the intention of going to the most extreme and unrealistic place you can take it, the absurdity can assist you in regaining a more rational way of thinking.

3-MINUTE CATASTROPHE

CATASTROPHIZING PROMPTS

- **Describe the situation with as much detail and emotion behind it as possible.**
- **What will this look like?**
- **How will you feel?**
- **Who will be impacted by this?**
  - How will they react to you?
  - What will happen to your relationship?
- **After each statement ask yourself then what will happen?**
  - And what will that mean if it does happen?
- **How will you see yourself after this situation or event?**

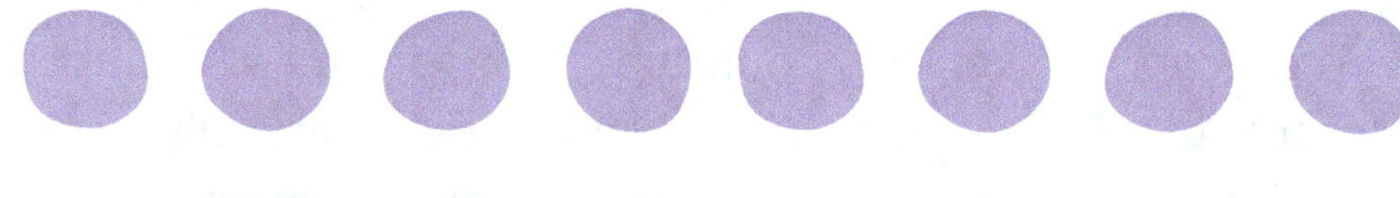

3-MINUTE CATASTROPHY

"If I don't pass this test, I will fail. I'm never going to make it. I'm going to end up being a bum and homeless, asking for items off the dollar menu."

"My boyfriend isn't answering my text messages. He's probably out with some other girl. Oh no, what if he is in love with another girl? He's never going to answer me. He's ghosting me. He never really loved me anyways. These past four years he's just been using me. I'm going to be all alone, FOREVER!"

REVIEW

PROS OF THIS WEEK'S SKILL

____

____

____

CONS OF THIS WEEK'S SKILL

____

____

____

WOO – HOO OF THE WEEK

____

____

____

REACTIONS TO THIS WEEK'S SKILL

____

____

____

____

____

____

____

DIFFICULTY OF SKILL

(1) (2) (3) (4) (5) (6) (7)

USEFULNESS OF SKILL

(1) (2) (3) (4) (5) (6) (7)

OVERALL MOOD THIS WEEK

NOTES

____

____

THOUGHT DUMPING

This week you will be thought dumping. This unstructured, freestyle method of journaling allows you to openly express your thoughts and feelings.

Dumping your thoughts onto paper does not have to look neat and organized. It does not have to make sense or even be legible. There is no right or wrong way to do a thought dump. The effect comes from the release, both the physical release of handwriting the thoughts and the emotional release of getting them from head to hand to paper.

Yes, handwritten, pen to paper! Research has shown this method to be cathartic for emotional release.

If you have a hard time getting started, you could even start with "I really don't want to do this. It is such a dumb idea to write this stuff down. . ." Just write whatever comes to mind from, "I can't stand this job anymore," to, "I really wish I had some chips and guacamole."

Allow your feelings to guide you and just write. So let it just drive until it runs out of steam. Eventually, you will be out of thoughts, or your hand will cramp. After you are unable to think of anything to add to your journaling put the pen down, take a deep inhale and exhale, and close the journal.

THOUGHT DUMPING

Give yourself at least five minutes before even thinking of reading it again. Just sit in the effects of releasing all the stagnant, pent-up energy that was deep within you. You may choose to go back and read what you wrote which may allow you to see some irrational thoughts and you could challenge those. It could also help you see patterns to your thinking or discover something that has been upsetting you for a while that perhaps you have pushed away. And if you decide to not read it then that's fine too. The point is to feel lighter at the end of this exercise.

Benefits:
- *Slows down racing thoughts.*
- *Quiets the overthinking parts of your brain or the monkey mind as some call it.*
- *Alleviates upsetting feelings.*
- *Helps identify unhelpful thinking patterns and irrational thoughts.*
- *Promotes feeling grounded and secure through self-soothing and self-validation.*

THOUGHT DUMPING

DUMP HERE!

WEEKLY

REVIEW

PROS OF THIS WEEK'S SKILL

____

____

____

CONS OF THIS WEEK'S SKILL

____

____

____

WOO – HOO OF THE WEEK

____

____

____

____

REACTIONS TO THIS WEEK'S SKILL

____

____

____

____

____

____

____

DIFFICULTY OF SKILL

(1) (2) (3) (4) (5) (6) (7)

USEFULNESS OF SKILL

(1) (2) (3) (4) (5) (6) (7)

OVERALL MOOD THIS WEEK

NOTES

____

____

BOX OF EXPECTATIONS

This week's skill is utilizing the Box of Expectations and identifying "should" statements.

Consider a person you have a relationship with, an upcoming event or yourself. You are to write all the things you think that person or event should be. How should they act? How should the event go? What should happen or not happen? What should be said or not said? Write all these expectations caused by "should" statements within the box provided for you.

After creating your box of expectations, ask yourself which of these qualities, traits, or characteristics does the person, or the situation have. Circle the ones that are accurate to the person or event.

On the outside of the box write down any other traits or characteristics that you appreciate about the person or event that are not included in your belief of how it should be.

When reviewing this exercise take into consideration the reality of this person or event meeting your expectations. If you were unable to circle all or most of the items listed in the box then perhaps it is worth asking if adjusting your expectations of the person and creating a box which does fit them would help ease your own upsetting feelings.

"Should" statements can cause some of the most debilitating anxiety. The expectations and restrictions placed on yourself, others, and the world with "should" statements can leave you feeling stuck to the point of almost paralyzing yourself.

BOX OF EXPECTATIONS

These statements may not be true or accurate, but by using the word "should" a rigid view is created which does not allow for flexibility or wiggly room. You may find yourself behaving in ingenuine ways due to your beliefs of how you "should" behave or present to others.

Benefits:
- *When these thoughts are challenged one can experience a decrease in feelings such as anxiety, depression, and self-doubt.*
- *Develop realistic expectations for self and others.*
- *Alleviate patterns of perfectionism and promote self-acceptance.*

How I Should Be . . .

Everyone should like me.
I should get along with everyone.
I should be able to work full time, work out, and eat healthy every day.
I should be able to keep my partner happy.

A Partner Should Be . . .

Thoughtful
Funny
Punctual
Like the same things as me.
They should want to change.
They should know when I am upset.

BOX OF EXPECTATIONS

REVIEW

PROS OF THIS WEEK'S SKILL

____

____

____

CONS OF THIS WEEK'S SKILL

____

____

____

WOO – HOO OF THE WEEK

____

____

____

____

REACTIONS TO THIS WEEK'S SKILL

____

____

____

____

____

____

____

____

DIFFICULTY OF SKILL

(1) (2) (3) (4) (5) (6) (7)

USEFULNESS OF SKILL

(1) (2) (3) (4) (5) (6) (7)

OVERALL MOOD THIS WEEK

NOTES

____

____

THROW OUT THE CRYSTAL BALL

This week you will learn to envision your very own crystal ball as a visualization method to combating one of the most common cognitive distortions, *Fortune Telling*. (See Unhelpful Styles of Thinking in appendix on page 189.)

- **Identify the prediction of how something may happen or how someone is going to respond.**
- **Now close your eyes and visualize yourself holding a crystal ball.**
- **Create a full vision of your scene and place it into the crystal ball.**
- **Take a deep breath and as I say to my clients "throw that crystal ball you are carrying around out the window!"**
- **Release the prediction and return to the present!**

It is human nature to want to know what is going to happen and be prepared to handle what is next. However, unless you have some unknown powers, it is unlikely your prediction is 100% accurate. Usually, these predictive behaviors lead to feelings of worry, anxiety, and even dread. Living in that place of prediction takes you away from being in the present moment and even your chance at experiencing contentment and happiness.

Remember you:
CANNOT predict people's behaviors.
CANNOT predict the outcomes of events.
CANNOT read people's minds.
CANNOT predict what someone is going to say.

THROW OUT THE CRYSTAL BALL

WHAT'S IN YOUR CRYSTAL BALL?

REVIEW

PROS OF THIS WEEK'S SKILL

____

____

____

CONS OF THIS WEEK'S SKILL

____

____

____

WOO – HOO OF THE WEEK

____

____

____

____

REACTIONS TO THIS WEEK'S SKILL

____

____

____

____

____

____

____

DIFFICULTY OF SKILL

① ② ③ ④ ⑤ ⑥ ⑦

USEFULNESS OF SKILL

① ② ③ ④ ⑤ ⑥ ⑦

OVERALL MOOD THIS WEEK

NOTES

____

____

THOUGHT REFRAMING

This week you will learn how to examine and reframe stress-inducing thoughts with the use of the included Thought Reframing Guide.

Let's recall the knowledge about cognitive distortions from your previous work. Remember the stinking thinking patterns? (Refer to appendix page 189 Unhelpful Styles of Thinking from Change Your Thoughts, Skill 1).

Start by identifying an unhelpful thought that promotes anxiety or stress for you. Then examine the thought and recognize if it is a cognitive distortion. And then develop a more helpful thought by using evidence and facts you identify. Use these facts to help disprove your unhelpful thought. Facts may include something that was said, or done, such as a behavior. Evidence may be recognizing patterns of on-going behaviors or events that have taken place.

Questions to Help in Examining Thoughts:
- *How accurate is this thought? Scoring from 0-100 (0, entirely untrue and 100, is completely true).*
- *What are some other possible views of the situation or event?*
- *How would _____ (fill the blank in with a close friend or relative that has a different perspective on things) view the situation?*
- *Is there anything that you can realistically do to influence the situation?*
- *What aspects of the situation do you have control over?*

THOUGHT REFRAMING

Benefits:
- *Assists in identifying automatic thoughts which contribute to low moods or sabotaging behaviors.*
- *Promotes neuroplasticity leading to changes in thought patterns over time.*
- *Increases self-esteem and self-confidence.*
- *Promotes the development of rational thinking patterns and efficiency in emotional regulation.*
- *Enables your ability to control your own thoughts and feelings.*

Thought Reframing Example:
Ian says to his therapist "there's no point in even going on the date, she probably won't even show and if she does, she won't like me." This is an example of fortune telling. Ian's therapist may respond by pointing out to him that he has no proof either of those things will happen. In fact, if he has already asked her out on the date and she said yes to it, this shows a level of interest in getting to know him further.

By helping Ian see some of the facts he is given the opportunity to rethink his thoughts about attending his date and perhaps change his perspective all together to something more accurate. A more accurate thought maybe, "I'm nervous to go on this date and get to know this woman. I'm grateful she was open to getting together and trying to get to know each other more."

THOUGHT REFRAMING

YOUR THOUGHT

____

IDENTIFY THE COGNITIVE DISTORTION

- [ ] **ALL OR NOTHING**

- [ ] **OVERGENERALIZING**

- [ ] **MIND-READING**

- [ ] **FORTUNE TELLING**

- [ ] **CATASTROPHIZING / MINIMIZING**

- [ ] **MENTAL FILTER**

- [ ] **EMOTIONAL REASONING**

- [ ] **SHOULD / MUST / OUGHT STATEMENT**

- [ ] **PERSONALIZATION**

THOUGHT REFRAMING

LIST YOUR FACTS & EVIDENCE

NEW THOUGHT

REVIEW

PROS OF THIS WEEK'S SKILL

____

____

____

CONS OF THIS WEEK'S SKILL

____

____

____

WOO – HOO OF THE WEEK

____

____

____

____

REACTIONS TO THIS WEEK'S SKILL

____

____

____

____

____

____

____

____

DIFFICULTY OF SKILL

(1) (2) (3) (4) (5) (6) (7)

USEFULNESS OF SKILL

(1) (2) (3) (4) (5) (6) (7)

OVERALL MOOD THIS WEEK

NOTES

____

THE TWO WEEK RULE

The next skill isn't a difficult skill to use but it is a challenge to develop. When you find yourself upset, stressed out, or obsessing about something, this little trick is so useful. Ask yourself, "Will this matter in two weeks?"

Guess what, nine times out of ten it won't even matter in two days, sometimes even two hours. Therefore, it most likely won't be of any significance in two weeks. That means it is not worth holding on to!

This technique creates a gentle shift in your mindset and teaches you acceptance. Learning acceptance can save you a ton of time and energy on something that you previously would have ruminated *(thinking over and over)* on.

The next time you catch yourself getting upset over something and you just can't seem to shake it ask yourself will it matter two weeks from now. If the answer is no . . .
LET IT GO!

WEEKLY
REVIEW

PROS OF THIS WEEK'S SKILL

____

____

____

CONS OF THIS WEEK'S SKILL

____

____

____

WOO – HOO OF THE WEEK

____

____

____

____

REACTIONS TO THIS WEEK'S SKILL

____

____

____

____

____

____

____

____

DIFFICULTY OF SKILL

(1) (2) (3) (4) (5) (6) (7)

USEFULNESS OF SKILL

(1) (2) (3) (4) (5) (6) (7)

OVERALL MOOD THIS WEEK

NOTES

____

____

MAKE IT ABSURD

This week's coping skill is a little unconventional when you first hear it but try to be open to the possibility. You know the term mountain out of a mole hill, well that is exactly what you will be doing this week. Take a worry or concern and completely blow it out of proportion. Let your imagination go wild, blow it out of the water and be completely absurd.

Give yourself a time limit, maybe 5-7 minutes if you are going to do this verbally or 7-12 minutes if you plan to write for this exercise.

How does this work? Eventually, your imagination will get to such an unlikely story that you have no choice but to chuckle and say there is no way that is going to happen. It then allows you to pull out those grounding techniques and come back down to Earth. Here on Earth, you will be able to reconnect with a more level-headed thought pattern and address the issue more realistically and from less of an emotional mentality.

When you find yourself ruminating or obsessing about something go for the worst-case scenario and then try to kick it up a notch. I dare you to!

MAKE IT ABSURD

JOURNAL HERE

WEEKLY

REVIEW

PROS OF THIS WEEK'S SKILL

____

____

____

CONS OF THIS WEEK'S SKILL

____

____

____

WOO – HOO OF THE WEEK

____

____

____

____

REACTIONS TO THIS WEEK'S SKILL

____

____

____

____

____

____

____

____

DIFFICULTY OF SKILL

(1) (2) (3) (4) (5) (6) (7)

USEFULNESS OF SKILL

(1) (2) (3) (4) (5) (6) (7)

OVERALL MOOD THIS WEEK

NOTES

____

____

BE PRESENT & MINDFUL

MINDFULNESS & GROUNDING TECHNIQUES

MINDFULMOMENTSLLC.COM

DESCRIBE 5 THINGS

This week you will practice describing five things you see with mindful observation.

- **Start by observing one item in your immediate area or within you for more of a challenge. You could choose to focus on a plant sitting on your windowsill or you could choose to bring your awareness to your legs resting against the couch you are sitting on.**
- **Now sit with this for a minute or two and just observe what is happening at this moment.**
- **As you settle into observing, allow yourself to remain present with the object or thing until your mind no longer allows it.**
- **Visually exploring the item and describing it to yourself. Allow any energetic connection between yourself and this thing come to be without questioning it or analyzing the connection.**
- **When you have reached the end of the first observation move on to the next.**

One of the fastest and most accessible grounding and mindfulness skills you can use is observation. By observing the present moment, you are becoming more aware of yourself and your surroundings. Observation uses the mind body connection to help promote a sense of presences and stillness. Learn to pause for a few minutes and just notice. Notice the present moment without judgment, that means no use of labels. Using just adjectives to describe whatever you may be noticing in the moment.

DESCRIBE 5 THINGS

Benefits:
- *Promotes self-awareness and mindfulness.*
- *Reduces anxiety and distressing thoughts.*
- *With practice becomes more natural and easier to redirect yourself back to present moment.*

Describe Five Things Example:
In my office I used to have this large chair, that had two shades of blue, orange, and yellow fabric. The dark blue portions of the chair were a soft texture, like crushed velvet and the rest was a rough material. So, as I would have sessions, I often would run a finger along the dark blue portion to help keep me present in the moment if ever I found my mind wandering. I would notice how the cushion conformed to my legs as I sat in the chair. I could feel the light wind coming through the window of my office. And I would feel the warm beam of sunlight against my arm as I sat in that chair.

REVIEW

PROS OF THIS WEEK'S SKILL

____

____

____

CONS OF THIS WEEK'S SKILL

____

____

____

WOO – HOO OF THE WEEK

____

____

____

____

REACTIONS TO THIS WEEK'S SKILL

____

____

____

____

____

____

____

____

DIFFICULTY OF SKILL

1 2 3 4 5 6 7

USEFULNESS OF SKILL

1 2 3 4 5 6 7

OVERALL MOOD THIS WEEK

NOTES

____

ENHANCING YOUR MINDFULNESS

Discovering mindfulness can be a little tricky at times, so for this week you will practice three mindfulness techniques of your choosing.

Some of the following techniques will require you to let go of a judgment that these are silly, pointless, or never going to work.

Mindfulness Techniques to Consider:
- **Play with silly putty** – this childhood favorite helps soothe you when stretching it. The putty will warm up and begin to stretch out further. The repetitive motion of stretching it becomes soothing as does the feeling of all the different textures and temperatures of the putty.
- **Hold an ice cube in your hand** – focus on the sensation of the coldness to your skin. Feel the ice begin to melt and turn back into water. Again, this is about observation, describe it without judgment.
- **Take a cold shower or warm bath** – connect to the way the water hits your body, the rise or fall of your own body temperature in relation to the shower or bath. If you can take a bubble bath maybe notice the way the bubbles conform to your body or the smell that accompanies the bubbles.
- **Rub your hands together creating friction** – notice as your hands begin to warm up and then place them over your eyelids for a soothing sensation.
- **Pet a pet** – spend a few minutes petting your personal pet or even a stuffed animal. The repetitive motion becomes soothing as does companionship, that energetic connection of being fully present with your animal.

Continued on next page

ENHANCING YOUR MINDFULNESS

- **Turn on some tunes** – any type of music whether instrumental or not can also help improve your mindfulness. Feel the vibration of the sounds, listen to the tempo and tones.
- **Taste for the experience** – one of my favorite mindfulness exercises is teaching people about the three bites. Grab your favorite snack and mindfully observe the snack, smell it before taking the first bite. Close your eyes and take a bite, notice all the flavor that rushes through your mouth. After the first bite do the same exercise for bite 2 and 3. Notice any changes in the intensity of the flavor. Finally go for a 4th bite, you may be surprised that the flavor remains the same as bite number 3. You really will be able to only have 3 bites of that cake next time at the party!
- **Burn a candle or incense** – aromatherapy has become more popular, and many companies sell essential oils. These, as well as the old fashion burning of candles can help fill your home with relaxing and comforting smells. Take a minute to just sit in the scent and allow yourself to feel the effects of the aromas.

These techniques can help you regain your sense of presence in the here and now. These suggestions may not all resonate with you or tickle your fancy but allow yourself to explore. See which senses you connect with the most and maybe explore other mindfulness techniques related to those senses.

The path to feeling mindful must come naturally. It's like looking for your lost keys, the harder you look for them the more they seem to evade you. Using your senses with an intention of being fully engaged in the present moment and releasing your expectations of what that moment should look like or feel like enhances your mindfulness practice.

ENHANCING YOUR MINDFULNESS

Benefits:

- *Enhances self-awareness and insight.*
- *Slows down the perception of time and improve time management skills.*
- *Reduces anxiety and stress.*
- *Improves focus and concentration.*
- *Decreases reactive responses to feelings and enhances ability to respond effectively to feelings.*

WEEKLY

REVIEW

PROS OF THIS WEEK'S SKILL

CONS OF THIS WEEK'S SKILL

WOO – HOO OF THE WEEK

REACTIONS TO THIS WEEK'S
SKILL

DIFFICULTY OF SKILL

(1) (2) (3) (4) (5) (6) (7)

USEFULNESS OF SKILL

(1) (2) (3) (4) (5) (6) (7)

OVERALL MOOD THIS WEEK

NOTES

PLANT YOUR FEET

This is honestly one of my favorites. Plant your feet!

You may have heard of earthing. Earthing is slightly more specific in that you would stand on the earth, grass, sand, whatever barefoot. This method, however, allows you to just use any surface for standing.

Place your feet firm to the ground either barefoot or with shoes on. You will be concentrating on feeling the energetic connection to the ground.

In times of high anxiety and ruminating thoughts you may want to stomp one foot down and then the other. Focus on the vibration through your feet and legs when you contact the ground. While standing with intention, breathe deeply and focus on rooting into the ground with your feet. Feel all four corners of your feet connect to the ground. Even if wearing shoes notice any sensations of the sole of your foot making contact to the bottom of your shoe.

By concentrating on your posture, your connection, and the exchange of energy you will find your mind slowing down. Your breathing will start to ease and become less shallow. The goal is to bring yourself back to a place of presence and mindfulness.

This is a wonderful skill to try in various settings. Try it at home, try it at work, or give it a shot while waiting at the grocery store. Once you get the hang of it you will find yourself doing it at random without necessarily being in distress.

PLANT YOUR FEET

Benefits:
- *Increases self-awareness.*
- *Enhances mindfulness practice.*
- *Creates a sensation of calm and feeling grounded.*
- *Promotes calmer, more relaxed breath patterns.*
- *Improves sleep.*
- *Decreases inflammation in the body.*

WEEKLY

REVIEW

PROS OF THIS WEEK'S SKILL

____

____

____

CONS OF THIS WEEK'S SKILL

____

____

____

WOO – HOO OF THE WEEK

____

____

____

____

REACTIONS TO THIS WEEK'S SKILL

____

____

____

____

____

____

____

____

DIFFICULTY OF SKILL

① ② ③ ④ ⑤ ⑥ ⑦

USEFULNESS OF SKILL

① ② ③ ④ ⑤ ⑥ ⑦

OVERALL MOOD THIS WEEK

NOTES

____

THE POWER OF SOUND HEALING

This week is focused on the power of sound and music. You will be trying different methods of sound healing this week.

Perhaps try a different genre of music while you work out or walk. Or find a video online or through one of the many popular meditation apps. It is alright if you try one and think "this isn't my jam." But don't just quit, try three or four different types of sound for yourself. And at the end of the week, review for yourself what you enjoyed and what you did not enjoy.

Other Types of Sound Healing:
- *Binaural Beats* - Binaural beats are a great tool to help induce a deeper state of sleep and rest at night. Their frequency is believed to activate the delta waves in your brain which are the brain waves that promote a better night's rest. There are other sound frequencies used for promoting healing of the chakra system or other intentions, such as surrendering fear.
- *Singing Bowls* - Singing bowls create a vibration which again taps into the mind-body connection. These bowls also stimulate areas of the brain. Sometimes when attending a session, the guide will have several singing bowls which align with your chakra system.
- *Tuning Forks* – Tuning forks are placed on to a joint or muscle. The vibration of the tuning fork is soothing and helps promote healing powers.

THE POWER OF SOUND HEALING

Benefits:
- *Re-connects the mind and body.*
- *Effectively treats depression, dementia, and stroke victims.*
- *Stimulates parts of the brain which helps calm the mind and reduces impulsivity.*
- *Reduces stress.*
- *Fewer mood swings.*
- *Lowers blood pressure and cholesterol levels.*
- *Improves sleep.*

REVIEW

PROS OF THIS WEEK'S SKILL

____

____

____

CONS OF THIS WEEK'S SKILL

____

____

____

WOO – HOO OF THE WEEK

____

____

____

____

REACTIONS TO THIS WEEK'S SKILL

____

____

____

____

____

____

____

____

____

DIFFICULTY OF SKILL

(1) (2) (3) (4) (5) (6) (7)

USEFULNESS OF SKILL

(1) (2) (3) (4) (5) (6) (7)

OVERALL MOOD THIS WEEK

NOTES

____

ROOT TO RISE GROUNDING

This week's skill focuses on grounding through mindful meditation. Find a comfortable seat and allow me to guide you to a place of peace and unity.

Follow the guided meditation included in the appendix on page 191 or you can find a recording of this meditation at www.youtube.com/@LetGoLetBe.

This is a lengthier practice to assist you in learning the posture in grounding work. After finishing this exercise, you may notice yourself sitting up taller or your core is more engaged. Or you may find that you feel slightly lightheaded. These reactions are perfectly normal, just notice them without judgment as they will pass.

After some practice you will find that you can ground yourself faster and more efficiently. This skill can be done whenever you take a moment for yourself to sit down. Before your morning coffee, before starting work, sitting at the park watching the ducks swim, or before a big test.

Benefits:
- *Helps maintain a stable mood.*
- *Increases mindfulness and a sense of being present in the here and now.*
- *Enhance your abilities to control your feelings.*

REVIEW

PROS OF THIS WEEK'S SKILL

____

____

____

CONS OF THIS WEEK'S SKILL

____

____

____

WOO – HOO OF THE WEEK

____

____

____

____

REACTIONS TO THIS WEEK'S SKILL

____

____

____

____

____

____

____

____

DIFFICULTY OF SKILL

① ② ③ ④ ⑤ ⑥ ⑦

USEFULNESS OF SKILL

① ② ③ ④ ⑤ ⑥ ⑦

OVERALL MOOD THIS WEEK

NOTES

____

____

INTENTIONAL MOVEMENT

This week try three different types of intentional movement for at least 10 minutes. This type of movement enhances the mind-body connection and aids in somatic healing.

To move with intention means to mindfully engage in the activity, so that one can release emotional blockages and reconnect the mind and body. This may allow an individual to feel their emotions in a safer and less threatening manner. No formal training is necessary as one can move with purpose even when taking a walk.

Throughout the years there has been a greater understanding of the mind-body connection and how the human body holds on to emotions. These emotions can manifest into physical problems, such as injury, tightness, or irritation. Research on trauma responses and physical symptoms shows that the body becomes impacted by psychological factors.

Benefits:
- *Increases mindfulness and the ability to be present with yourself.*
- *Aids in trauma recovery work as trauma can lead to dissociating, which is feeling disconnected from your body or the world around you.*
- *Stimulates parts of the brain that helps deactivate the "freeze" response of trauma.*
- *Stimulates the vagus nerve (the nerve responsible for calming you down) and releases endorphins.*

INTENTIONAL MOVEMENT

TYPES OF MOVEMENT

Yoga
Walking
Tai Chi
Hula Hoop (my personal favorite!)
Jumping Rope
Ice Skating
Dancing
Jumping on a Trampoline

Whatever type of movement you choose plan to do it mindfully and with the intention of being with yourself and in yourself.

REVIEW YOUR EXPERIENCES

- *What type of movements did you choose this week?*
  - *Were they more formal like taking a yoga class or informal like going for a walk?*
- *What did you notice during your movement?*
- *How did it feel when you first started the movement versus once it was done?*
- *Did you notice a change in yourself later in the day?*
  - *Did you feel more grounded or perhaps lighter?*

REVIEW

PROS OF THIS WEEK'S SKILL

____

____

____

CONS OF THIS WEEK'S SKILL

____

____

____

WOO – HOO OF THE WEEK

____

____

____

____

REACTIONS TO THIS WEEK'S SKILL

____

____

____

____

____

____

____

____

DIFFICULTY OF SKILL

① ② ③ ④ ⑤ ⑥ ⑦

USEFULNESS OF SKILL

① ② ③ ④ ⑤ ⑥ ⑦

OVERALL MOOD THIS WEEK

NOTES

____

LEARN TO SURRENDER
JOURNALING ACTIVITY

This week you will be working on learning to surrender through journaling.

- Identify or acknowledge what it is that needs to be let go of.
  - What are you holding onto? This can be an emotion, an unrealistic expectation, a perception of a past event, or your own negative beliefs about yourself, others, or the world.
- Consider what is the worst thing that could happen if you were to let go of this.
  - What would be the best-case scenario if you were to release this?
- Imagine the feeling that would fill you up if you were to release this.
  - What emotion do you attach to that? Keep that feeling in mind and give yourself permission to let go of the thing you have chosen to surrender. You may have to experience an array of emotions before allowing yourself to let go of the attachment to what you chose. That's okay, surrendering can be a journey, sometimes short or sometimes lengthy.
- Finally, surrender to a higher power. Trust that this thing has gone and no longer needs to be your concern. With trust and acceptance, it will work out as it needs to.
  - If you do not have a strong connection to a higher power allow yourself to further explore this within your journaling practices.

LEARN TO SURRENDER
JOURNALING ACTIVITY

The concept to surrender is often misunderstood. What do you think of when you hear the word surrender? Weak, to give-up and wave the white flag. This view of surrendering may leave a person feeling helpless, hopeless, or defeated.

True surrendering is an act of empowerment and realization. The skill of surrendering is built over time through mindfulness practices and various methods to help shift perspective, including this week's skill.

As you become more comfortable with surrendering, the process will come more naturally.

Surrendering the need to control anxiety, fear, and resentment, you will allow yourself to increase in faith, love, and happiness.

Benefits:
- *Promotes acceptance, peace, and relief.*
- *Releases the desire to control those things you cannot control.*
- *Helps in creating realistic expectations.*
- *Nurtures self-love and self-acceptance.*
- *Increases acceptance of others.*
- *To surrender permits you to stop fighting against your reality and empowers you to work with it instead of against it.*

SURRENDER
JOURNALING ACTIVITY

LEARNING TO LET GO

WEEKLY

REVIEW

PROS OF THIS WEEK'S SKILL

____

____

____

CONS OF THIS WEEK'S SKILL

____

____

____

WOO – HOO OF THE WEEK

____

____

____

____

REACTIONS TO THIS WEEK'S SKILL

____

____

____

____

____

____

____

____

DIFFICULTY OF SKILL

(1) (2) (3) (4) (5) (6) (7)

USEFULNESS OF SKILL

(1) (2) (3) (4) (5) (6) (7)

OVERALL MOOD THIS WEEK

☺ ☺ ☺ ☹ ☹ ☺ ☺

NOTES

____

____

5,4,3,2,1 GROUND

This week's skill is a popular grounding tool called 5, 4, 3, 2, 1, Ground. This is another skill that has you using your senses.

Identify the following:
- 5 things you see around you.
- 4 things you can touch.
- 3 things you can hear.
- 2 things you can smell.
- 1 thing you can taste.

Use descriptive words for each sense in this exercise.
- Sight – blue, orange, large, small, shiny, dull, sheer, shimmery, hazy, crinkled, crowded . . .
- Touch – smooth, jagged, bumpy, cold, warm, slimy, greasy, muggy, lumpy, uneven . . .
- Hear – swish, whoosh, fizz, humming, buzzing, gurgling, hissing, wheezy, soft, shrill . . .
- Smell – fresh, fishy, skunky, fruity, flowery, sour, musky, musty, fragrant, sweet, minty . . .
- Taste – sharp, tart, sour, acidic, sweet, bitter, buttery, salty, smokey, flavorful, plain . . .

Benefits:
- *Reduces anxiety and stress.*
- *Promotes a sense of feeling grounded and mindful.*
- *Reconnects the body and mind, promoting a sense of presences in the here and now.*

5,4,3,2,1 GROUND

ITEM I AM OBSERVING : The Couch

- Sight – Blue, long, rectangular, dark, bulky, wide, and wrinkly.

- Touch – bumpy, soft, and scratchy.

- Hear – plop when sitting on it and creaking.

- Smell – faint flowery scent.

- Taste – tasteless.

ITEM I AM OBSERVING :

- Sight –

- Touch –

- Hear –

- Smell –

- Taste –

REVIEW

PROS OF THIS WEEK'S SKILL

____

____

____

CONS OF THIS WEEK'S SKILL

____

____

____

WOO – HOO OF THE WEEK

____

____

____

____

REACTIONS TO THIS WEEK'S SKILL

____

____

____

____

____

____

____

____

DIFFICULTY OF SKILL

(1) (2) (3) (4) (5) (6) (7)

USEFULNESS OF SKILL

(1) (2) (3) (4) (5) (6) (7)

OVERALL MOOD THIS WEEK

NOTES

____

____

BE KIND TO YOURSELF & OTHERS

SELF-COMPASSION & ACCEPTANCE TECHNIQUES

LETTERS OF GRATITUDE

One of the biggest healing tools you can learn to implement is the power of gratitude. A fun exercise to promote gratitude is to write a letter of gratitude to someone you are grateful for. It can be someone that either is currently in your life or was a part of your life in the past.

Start by making a list of people you are grateful for knowing or have known. Select one person from the list to write a letter to expressing your gratitude towards them. The letter never has to be mailed if you do not wish to send it. You may decide to continue with this practice on a weekly or month basis for yourself.

Want a little challenge? Try writing a letter of gratitude towards yourself!

Benefits:
- *Gratitude is a mood enhancer.*
- *Increases positive thinking and promotes a positive mindset.*
- *Improves your relationship with yourself and others.*
- *Gratitude practices promote more gratitude and a feeling of abundance.*

REVIEW

PROS OF THIS WEEK'S SKILL

____

____

____

CONS OF THIS WEEK'S SKILL

____

____

____

WOO – HOO OF THE WEEK

____

____

____

____

REACTIONS TO THIS WEEK'S SKILL

____

____

____

____

____

____

____

DIFFICULTY OF SKILL

(1) (2) (3) (4) (5) (6) (7)

USEFULNESS OF SKILL

(1) (2) (3) (4) (5) (6) (7)

OVERALL MOOD THIS WEEK

NOTES

____

____

MY BEST SELF

This week is a journaling activity to help build and maintain your self-esteem. Reflect on the best version of yourself.

Take some time to journal about a time in your life that you felt in-sync with your beliefs, your goals, and principles. Periodically throughout this week take five to ten minutes to reflect on some or all the journaling prompts included in this week's skill.

Most likely you are your toughest critic! The danger of on-going self-judgement and criticism is the impact it has on your self-esteem and self-worth. Reminding yourself of actual events that demonstrate qualities you appreciate about yourself and hold in high regard can help combat self-criticism and judgement.

Benefits:

- *Improves self-esteem and self-worth through practicing self-validation.*
- *Aides in neuroplasticity, the rewiring of your brain to think in more positive patterns.*
- *Increases mindfulness skills and a sense of presence and acceptance with the self.*

MY BEST SELF

JOURNAL PROMPTS

- **Describe a time you were faced with a difficult decision that you decided to take action and worked in your favor.**
  - *How did you make that decision?*
  - *How did you feel after seeing the situation through?*
- **Describe an experience that left you feeling proud and confident.**
  - *What about this experience brought you joy?*
  - *Was there anything about the experience that surprised you for the good?*
- **Describe a relationship in which you felt deeply loved and loving towards the other person.**
  - *How does this relationship impact your view of yourself and the world overall?*
  - *Were there any challenges along the way of developing this type of relationship? How were those challenges resolved?*
- **Describe a time that you felt a sense of acceptance with yourself.**
  - *What type of feelings did you experience during this time?*
  - *Were these feelings evident at the time or did you notice them in retrospect?*
- **If your best self could write you a pep talk, what would he/she/they say today?**

MY BEST SELF

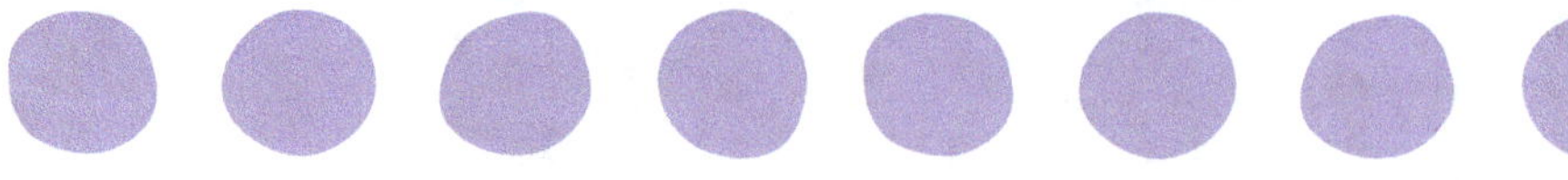

REVIEW

PROS OF THIS WEEK'S SKILL

____

____

____

CONS OF THIS WEEK'S SKILL

____

____

____

WOO – HOO OF THE WEEK

____

____

____

____

REACTIONS TO THIS WEEK'S SKILL

____

____

____

____

____

____

____

____

DIFFICULTY OF SKILL

(1) (2) (3) (4) (5) (6) (7)

USEFULNESS OF SKILL

(1) (2) (3) (4) (5) (6) (7)

OVERALL MOOD THIS WEEK

NOTES

____

____

SELF-ESTEEM AND SELF-PRAISE

This week is about practicing self-praise. Self-praise allows you to acknowledge your strengths and positive qualities, as well as recognize any achievements and accomplishments you have made. Keeping a record of your personal Woo-Hoo's, as I like to call them helps build evidence and consistency in positive reflections of the self.

- **One way to do this activity is to keep a journal by your bed and as part of your nighttime routine identify three things you did well for the day, or brought you pride. Some days you may be proud of yourself for folding and putting away the laundry or taking a shower, while other days you will be praising yourself for having a hard conversation or presenting in front of a group. It's normal for it to vary on a day-to-day basis.**

- **Another fun way to do this exercise is by keeping a jar just full of Woo-Hoo's. Writing down what it is you are proud of and putting it into the jar allows you to pull one or two of these slips of paper out when having an off day. This doesn't hurt for a little mood booster!**

By acknowledging the Woo-Hoo moments in your day-to-day you will find your perception of yourself becomes healthier and more positive. Building a stronger sense of self provides confidence and self-encouragement which is part of building a healthy self-esteem.

SELF-ESTEEM AND SELF-PRAISE

Self-esteem is a big component to learning how to cope with emotional distress. Understand that self-esteem ebbs and flows and so will your comfort with managing upsetting feelings.

Higher levels of self-esteem result in increased self-love, self-worth, and self-confidence. With higher levels of these characteristics, you will be able to have a clearer picture of your own personal strengths and limitations resulting in realistic expectations in yourself.

SELF-ESTEEM AND SELF-PRAISE

YOUR PERSONAL WOO HOO'S

REVIEW

PROS OF THIS WEEK'S SKILL

____

____

____

CONS OF THIS WEEK'S SKILL

____

____

____

WOO – HOO OF THE WEEK

____

____

____

____

REACTIONS TO THIS WEEK'S SKILL

____

____

____

____

____

____

____

DIFFICULTY OF SKILL

1 2 3 4 5 6 7

USEFULNESS OF SKILL

1 2 3 4 5 6 7

OVERALL MOOD THIS WEEK

NOTES

____

____

A LETTER OF SELF-PRAISE

This week you will practice self-praise. Using a writing prompt write a letter praising yourself.

Too often you may find your inner critic screaming at you, which just leaves you filled with self-doubt, regret, or disappointment.

Start by focusing on what about you you're grateful for, such as characteristics, traits or even skills. Your letter does not have to be lengthy nor gushy unless that's your style. You can choose to do this exercise as many times as you wish. Again, three times does the charm!

Not up to the full letter writing, why not just write yourself small little notes to add to your pocket for the day that's praising you for a job well done? A pocket full of praise doesn't sound half bad now does it!

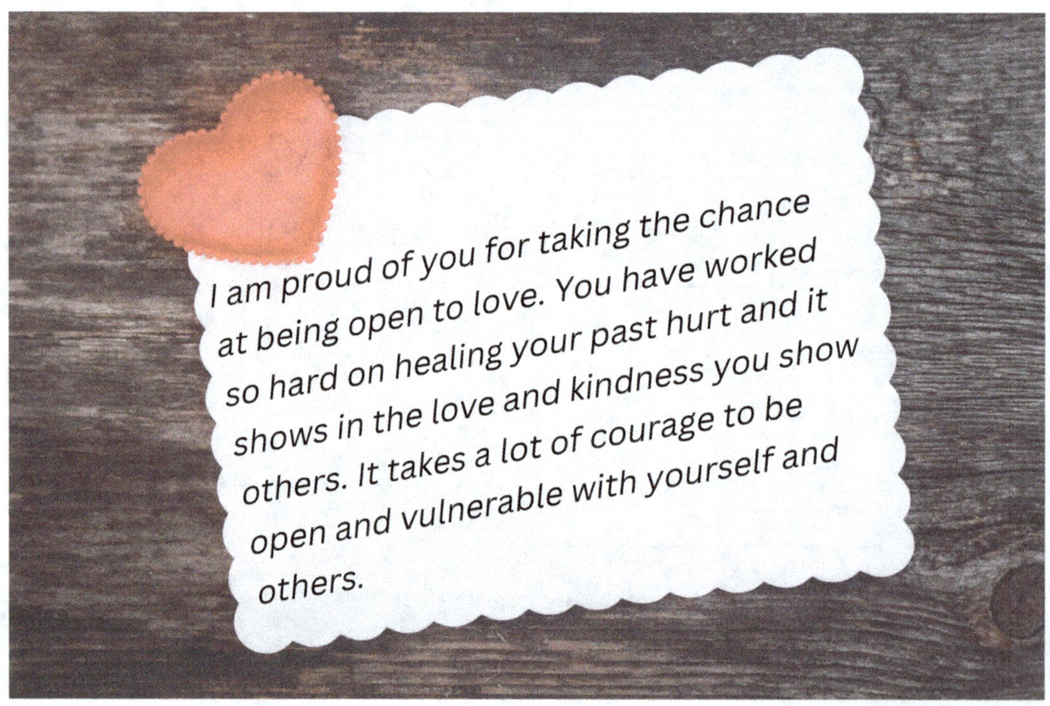

WEEKLY

REVIEW

PROS OF THIS WEEK'S SKILL

____

____

____

CONS OF THIS WEEK'S SKILL

____

____

____

WOO – HOO OF THE WEEK

____

____

____

____

REACTIONS TO THIS WEEK'S SKILL

____

____

____

____

____

____

____

____

____

DIFFICULTY OF SKILL

① ② ③ ④ ⑤ ⑥ ⑦

USEFULNESS OF SKILL

① ② ③ ④ ⑤ ⑥ ⑦

OVERALL MOOD THIS WEEK

NOTES

____

HUGS FOR A SMILE

Self-love with a hug! This week you are you to give yourself at least three 20-second or longer hugs.

Yes, even a self-hug can have a positive impact on your mood. And if you have people around you, perhaps, ask for a hug from them. Ask them if you can give them a hug. Spread the love and the joy by giving friends and family members hugs.

Take the skill a step further, experiment a little and see the actual power behind human contact and touch. Modern times has led to less face-to-face interaction. And even less physical contact with others.

Remember when you used to shake someone's hand when meeting them? Well, that handshake used to help break down a layer of defense and helped create a more positive interaction between you and the other person.

Benefits:
- *Receiving a hug increases positive feelings caused by a release of oxytocin and serotonin.*
- *A 20-second hug can help reduce symptoms of stress and anxiety.*
- *Reduces blood pressure and heart rate.*
- *Increases serotonin functioning which helps improve your mood and sleep.*

WEEKLY
REVIEW

PROS OF THIS WEEK'S SKILL

____

____

____

CONS OF THIS WEEK'S SKILL

____

____

____

WOO – HOO OF THE WEEK

____

____

____

____

REACTIONS TO THIS WEEK'S SKILL

____

____

____

____

____

____

____

DIFFICULTY OF SKILL

(1) (2) (3) (4) (5) (6) (7)

USEFULNESS OF SKILL

(1) (2) (3) (4) (5) (6) (7)

OVERALL MOOD THIS WEEK

NOTES

____

____

LETTER TO YOUR YOUNGER SELF

This week you will be writing a letter to your inner child from your adult self. Using the prompts provided for this week you will express compassion, encouragement, and acceptance towards your inner child. The healing of the inner child involves being able to be the caregiver that your younger self needed in the past. This is the same caregiver your adult self requires and deserves.

Just remember there is no right or wrong way to do this exercise, it is about self-expression. This can also stir up some old emotions, so it may lead you to needing to process this experience more. Processing can and should be done with a wellness professional of your choosing. Inner child work can be very powerful and healing and should not be taken lightly.

The inner child is a concept within psychology that helps individuals focus on healing the subconscious parts of the self that they have been carrying for years. The inner child develops in the earlier stages of life. The child has incorporated different messages and beliefs about the self which impact you as an adult today. This piece of the self may contain memories, emotions, childhood wounds, as well as hopes and dreams.

One's inner child is often activated when a need is not being met. A need like a need that was not properly met as a child. Typically, these needs are unconditional love, safety, and security. When not met, a child has no choice but to try and make sense of their world. The child will find a means of coping with the feelings associated with this unmet need. Coping can form in both adaptive and maladaptive methods.

LETTER TO YOUR YOUNGER SELF

Benefits:
- *Reconnecting to the inner child promotes healing and integration of the adult self and inner child.*
- *Increases awareness between past traumas and present-day behaviors.*
- *Helps in the development of healthy and adaptive coping mechanisms.*
- *Helps develop emotional regulation.*

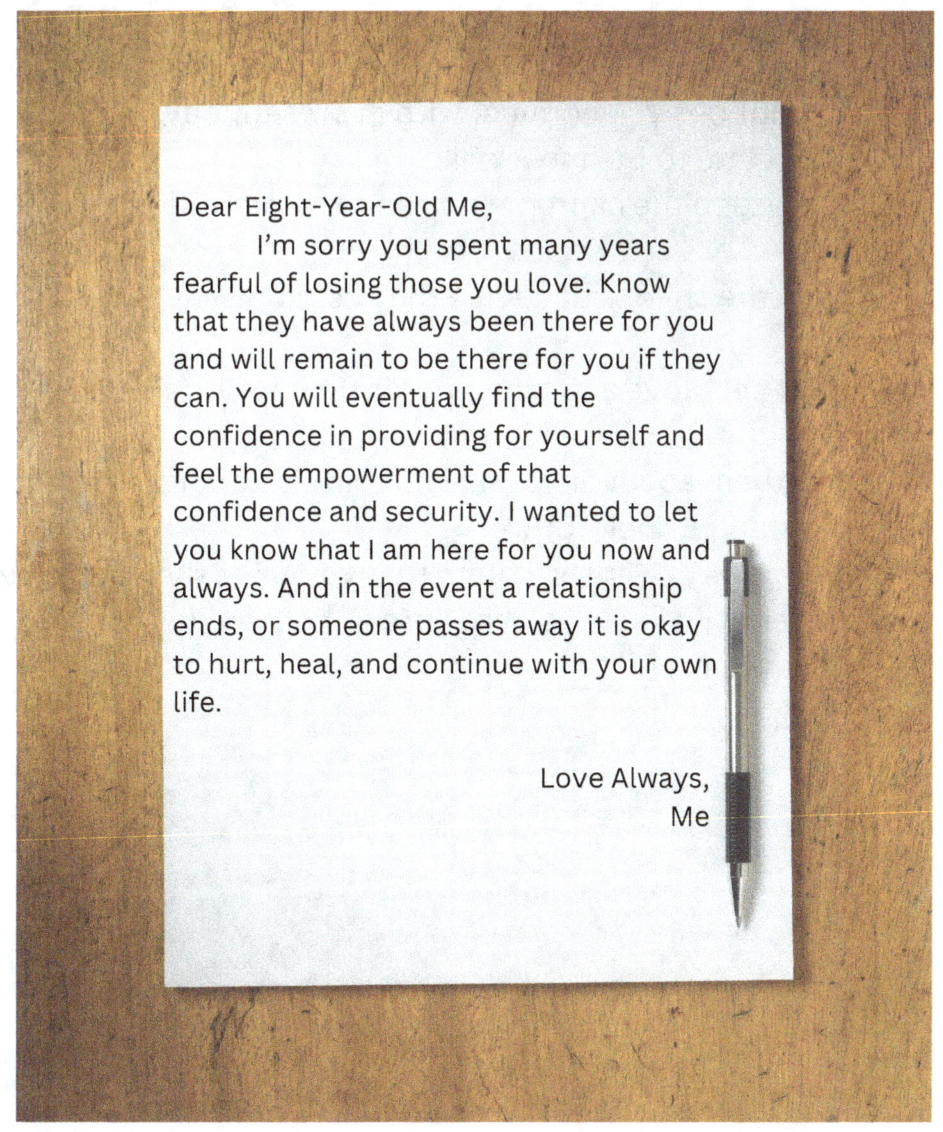

LETTER TO YOUR YOUNGER SELF

JOURNAL PROMPTS

- Pick an age in which you connect to as being significant.
- Acknowledge the child's struggles by validating it must have been tough not knowing how to cope with _______ (whatever experience you had at that age).
- Validate their emotional experience at the time and any of their emotions you connect with in present day. In other words, relate to the inner child.
- Emphasize to the child their strengths and resiliency they show.
- Provide the child with advice they could have used in the past.
- Express your love and concern for their well-being and safety.
- Inform them about anything you think is important for them to know about their future.
- Write in a way to ensure them that you have their back. Let the inner child know you are here to help guide them, to protect them, and to love them.

REVIEW

PROS OF THIS WEEK'S SKILL

____

____

____

CONS OF THIS WEEK'S SKILL

____

____

____

WOO – HOO OF THE WEEK

____

____

____

____

REACTIONS TO THIS WEEK'S SKILL

____

____

____

____

____

____

____

____

DIFFICULTY OF SKILL

(1) (2) (3) (4) (5) (6) (7)

USEFULNESS OF SKILL

(1) (2) (3) (4) (5) (6) (7)

OVERALL MOOD THIS WEEK

NOTES

____

____

SELF-TALK

This week's skill is positive self-talk (enter your eye-roll or groan here). Your positive self-talk practice will include repeating an affirmation while looking in the mirror.

- **Start by selecting either an affirmation you have come across or a personalized positive self-talk statement you have developed.** *Hint, hint, you could use your Personal Mantra from Calm Yourself, Skill 3 on page 6.*
- **Once you know what you will be saying, practice standing in front of the mirror and looking yourself in the eye.**
- **Begin to repeat your affirmation out loud. Repeat this statement at least 3-5 times and observe the change in your physical body and body language.**
- **Aim to practice this skill daily for this week. A great time to practice is either in the morning or the evening before bed.**

Looking yourself in the mirror may be challenging but is more effective in changing self-talk than just saying it out loud. By repeating this positive statement to yourself in the mirror you can see your body language. Your feelings are reflected to you through the mirror this will give you feedback. For instance, you will see resistance in yourself when using a statement that feels uncomfortable to believe or you may see joy and pride reflected as you believe in the statements you have decided to practice.

Positive self-talk is the most crucial coping skill you can build for yourself. It is the foundation to coping effectively and consistently with life stressors.

SELF-TALK

The trick to integrating positive self-talk into your belief system comes from receiving the same message over and over. Therefore, a child that receives negative messages about themselves over and over can internalize these messages and develop negative self-talk and low self-esteem. Negative self-talk can be one of the biggest sabotaging behaviors.

How does one combat the negative self-talk trap?

- By becoming more aware and catching when it's happening. A little trick for catching the negative self-talk is asking yourself "would I ever speak to my best-friend this way?" If the answer is no, then you best be changing what you are saying to yourself.

- When developing positive self-talk ask yourself, "what would I tell my best friend or my child?" Because I bet you treat them with a lot more compassion and encouragement than you treat yourself!

SELF-TALK

POSITIVE SELF-TALK STATEMENTS

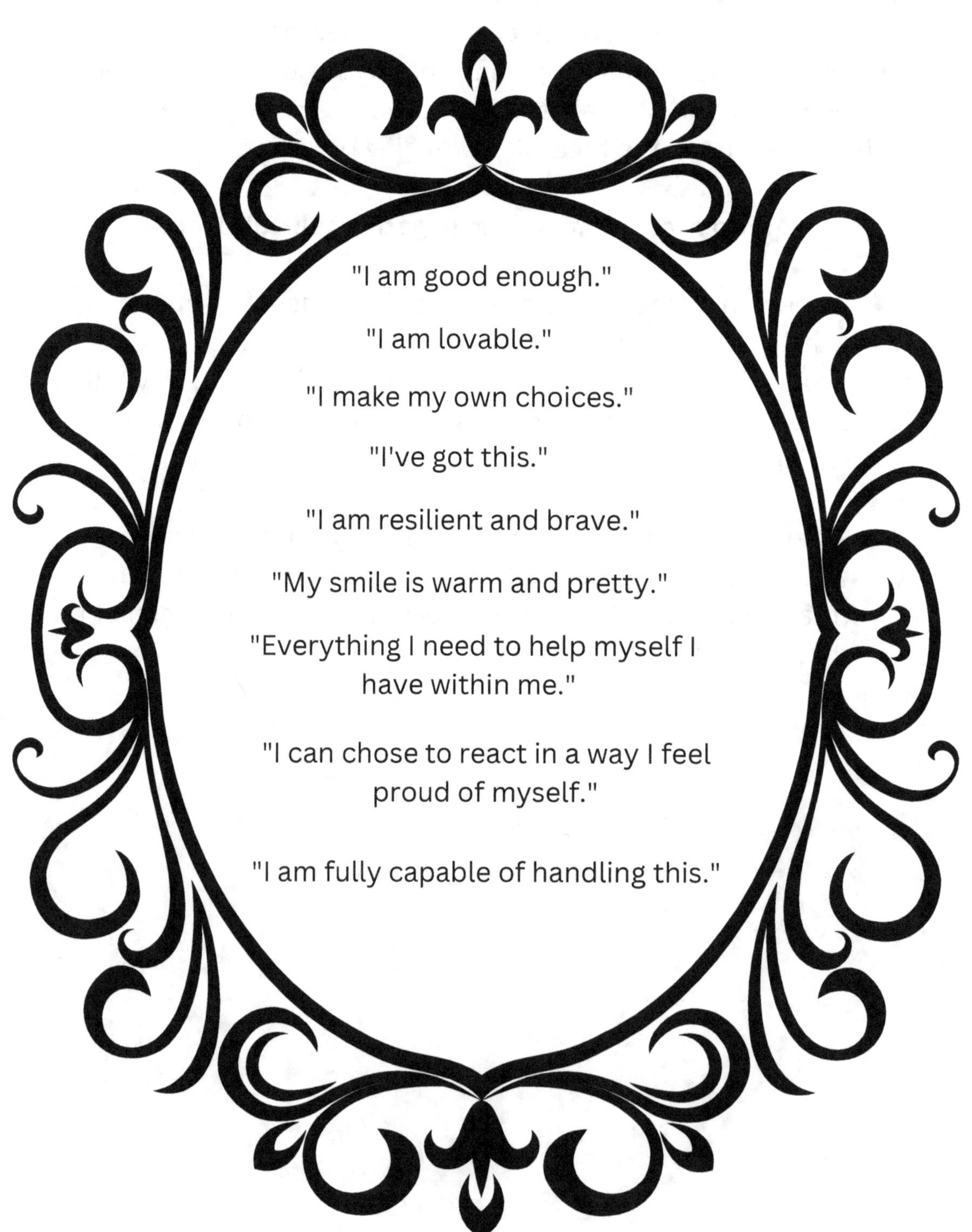

REVIEW

PROS OF THIS WEEK'S SKILL

____

____

____

CONS OF THIS WEEK'S SKILL

____

____

____

WOO – HOO OF THE WEEK

____

____

____

____

REACTIONS TO THIS WEEK'S SKILL

____

____

____

____

____

____

____

DIFFICULTY OF SKILL

(1) (2) (3) (4) (5) (6) (7)

USEFULNESS OF SKILL

(1) (2) (3) (4) (5) (6) (7)

OVERALL MOOD THIS WEEK

NOTES

____

____

LETTER OF FORGIVENESS

Big emotions like anger, resentment, hurt, and betrayal can impact you for years if left unhealed. This week you will be participating in a journaling activity focusing on forgiveness. The journal activity is to write a letter of forgiveness to someone who has hurt you in the past that you continue to carry hurt or resentment towards. This activity can be challenging.

Use the prompt page to assist you. If necessary, feel free to start with an easier task to forgive and work your way up to the hard and larger resentments.

Forgiveness is not an excuse for the wrong that was done, and it does not mean you forget what happened. It is about freeing yourself from the on-going pain associated with the hurt of what happened.

The act of forgiving is for you, the individual, rather than for the other person.

For example, how many times have you forgiven someone but never informed them that you forgave them. By forgiving them you probably found yourself feeling more at ease and your relationship with the other person probably returned to a more amicable state.

LETTER OF FORGIVENESS

Benefits:
- *Positive impact on mental and physical health.*
- *Increases sense of security and confidence.*
- *Forgiveness helps reduce cholesterol and blood pressure.*
- *Improves sleep patterns and quality.*
- *Helps lower the risk of heart attack.*
- *Practicing forgiveness lowers anxiety and depression in individuals.*
- *Promotes acceptance and mindfulness. It is important to note acceptance does not mean you agree with it or like it but understand that it is what it is, and it cannot be undone.*

LETTER OF FORGIVENESS

- **Working from a place of empathy, to see the situation through the other person's eyes can assist in forgiveness.**
  - Ask yourself if they intentionally set out to hurt you. Or did they hurt you because they were trying to meet their own needs or wants without recognizing the potential consequences of their behaviors?

- **Imagine what forgiveness may feel like for you.**
  - How would you act when the subject comes up in the future?
  - How would you respond to this person in the future?

- **Allow yourself to be imaginative and compassionate in your visualization of this new place of forgiveness.**

Bonus Work:

As forgiveness comes more naturally to you, you can work towards self-forgiveness.

The ultimate letter of forgiveness will be addressed to . . . YOURSELF!

That's right! Imagine freeing yourself from feelings of guilt, shame, and anger that you have carried with you for years.

REVIEW

PROS OF THIS WEEK'S SKILL

____

____

____

CONS OF THIS WEEK'S SKILL

____

____

____

WOO – HOO OF THE WEEK

____

____

____

____

REACTIONS TO THIS WEEK'S SKILL

____

____

____

____

____

____

____

____

DIFFICULTY OF SKILL

(1) (2) (3) (4) (5) (6) (7)

USEFULNESS OF SKILL

(1) (2) (3) (4) (5) (6) (7)

OVERALL MOOD THIS WEEK

NOTES

____

____

SELF-CARE

MAINTENANCE & RELAPSE PREVENTION SKILLS

FINDING BALANCE

You've probably been told more than once that the key to taking care of yourself is having balance, but no one seems to have a clear answer to what that is or looks like. This week you will journal about your own experience and hopes for a balanced lifestyle.

You will start with some questions to help you navigate this exercise. This will help you recognize where you may require more flexibility in your world to feel more balanced. In addition, you will be asked to describe what a more balanced life would look and feel like. Afterall, how are you to achieve something if you don't know what you are looking for?

One thing to keep in mind when searching for this sense of balance is that it is not always a 50/50 split. For instance, would it be more realistic if your work-life balance were a 35/65 split. And keep in mind this could shift during different times in your career or personal life.

Remember life is not just work and play! Consider all the roles you take on in your life. The juggling between roles is what makes up your balance. Accepting that balance and harmony are in a forever state of flux will help you achieve a place of calm and peacefulness.

FINDING BALANCE

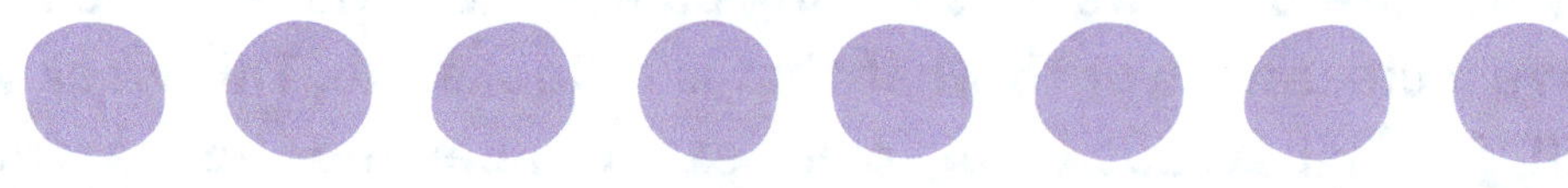

Use the following questions to help identify your roles, priorities, preferences, and responsibilities.

- **Briefly describe how you see balance currently in your life.**
- **What roles do you take on in your life?** *(i.e., mother/father, daughter/son, wife/husband, friend, co-worker, volunteer).*
- **What activities/hobbies/interests are you involved in?** *Rate these activities on their level of priority to you on a scale of 0-10 (10 being the highest priority).*
- **If you had to give up one of your hobbies/interests, which one would it be and why?**
- **What do you consider your responsibilities?** *(i.e., taking care of children or pets, cleaning your home).*
- **Talk a little bit about your job.**
  - *What do you do?*
  - *How demanding is the workplace?*
  - *How does your job leave you feeling at the end of a typical day?*
- **Describe your significant relationships and how they impact your sense of calm, peace, and balance?**
- **What would you like to see yourself doing more of in life?**
- **How could help from others change your ability to create more balance in your day to day?**

FINDING BALANCE

JOURNAL PROMPTS

Using the questions that you have explored take some time to freely write what you believe a more balanced way of living would look like for you.

Let's be realistic because most of us would love to say "Well, I win the lottery and buy an island off the coast of Italy where I just eat pasta every day and spend time with loved ones." Yep, that would be great but even in that scenario you still need to get your laundry done. So, be honest and realistic.

What would life look like if you were open to the ebb and flow of nature?

Can you imagine bringing a sense of harmony and balance to

FINDING BALANCE

JOURNAL HERE

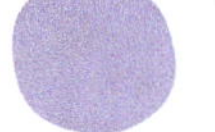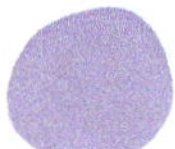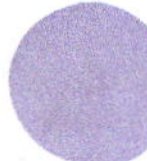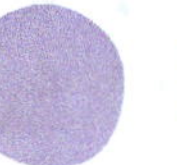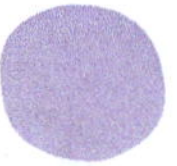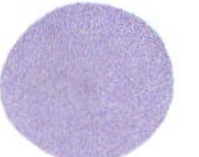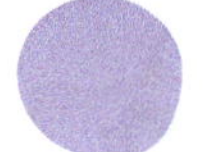

REVIEW

PROS OF THIS WEEK'S SKILL

____

____

____

CONS OF THIS WEEK'S SKILL

____

____

____

WOO – HOO OF THE WEEK

____

____

____

____

REACTIONS TO THIS WEEK'S SKILL

____

____

____

____

____

____

____

____

DIFFICULTY OF SKILL

(1) (2) (3) (4) (5) (6) (7)

USEFULNESS OF SKILL

(1) (2) (3) (4) (5) (6) (7)

OVERALL MOOD THIS WEEK

NOTES

____

____

SELF-CARE ON A BUDGET

This week you will focus on self-care. Using the Needs and Self-Care Inventory you will identify your personal needs and self-care to assist with meeting these needs that won't break the bank. Try to implement at least three of these acts of self-care over the next week.

Keep in mind your needs as these will help you discover new acts of self-care.
- **A need for mental clarity.**
- **A need for emotional release and soothing.**
- **A need to care for your physical being.**
- **A need for a safe and secure environment for oneself.**
- **A spiritual need to feel purposeful.**
- **A need for leisure and fun to help keep that jovial sense within you.**
- **A social need to be connected to others.**

There are so many ways to provide a little extra care for yourself that won't cost anything or cost very little. Setting limits to things that deplete your energy such as people, places, or activities. Participate in something that fulfills you. Self-care truly boils down to boundaries, compassion, and patience for oneself and one's needs.

How many times have you heard yourself saying I don't have the time for self-care, or I can't afford to do self-care? Do you have the time for self-neglect? In the long run self-neglect will cost you much more time and resources than integrating small, yet effective self-care measures.

SELF-CARE ON A BUDGET

Of course, the luxurious self-care sounds very nice but let's be real you're a busy individual that needs to optimize the time you have. And realistically you may or may not be working on a budget. But self-care does not have to be outrageous! Keep it to a manageable activity or decision, something that will set you up for success.

Benefits:
- *Enhances self-esteem.*
- *Increases productivity.*
- *Reduces stress and anxiety.*
- *Improves distress tolerance levels.*
- *Enhances interpersonal relationships.*

Self-Care Example:
- **Setting a boundary and turning off your work computer at a certain time each night.**
- **Spending an extra five minutes in the shower feeling the water hit the back of your neck and letting go of the tension of the day.**
- **Putting a facemask on after work.**
- **Getting up early and watching the sunrise or watching it set after work one night.**
- **Going for a walk on your lunch hour.**
- **Declining the invite to dinner on Thursday evening.**

SELF-CARE ON A BUDGET

NEEDS & CARE INVENTORY

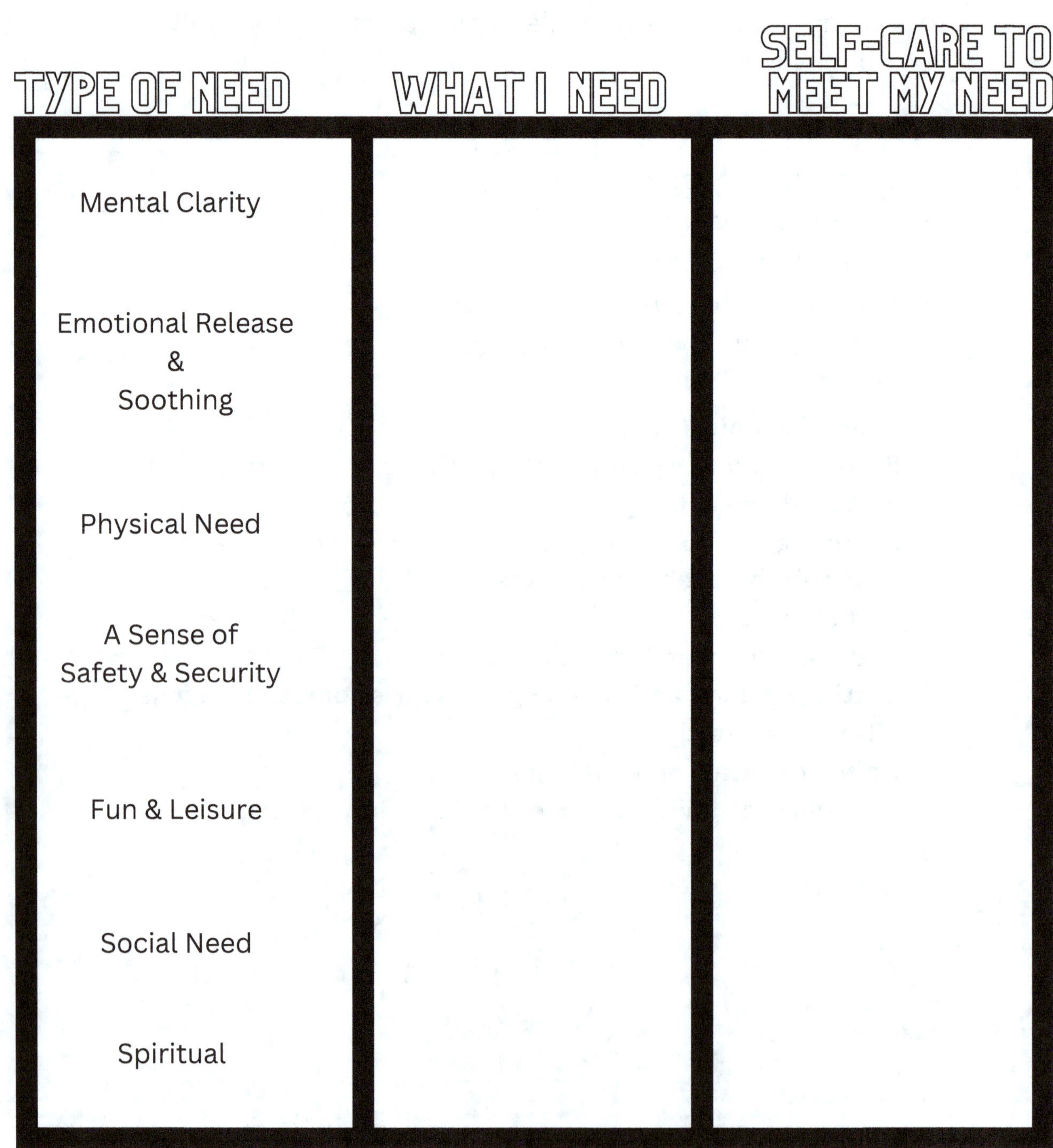

TYPE OF NEED	WHAT I NEED	SELF-CARE TO MEET MY NEED
Mental Clarity		
Emotional Release & Soothing		
Physical Need		
A Sense of Safety & Security		
Fun & Leisure		
Social Need		
Spiritual		

WEEKLY
REVIEW

PROS OF THIS WEEK'S SKILL

____

____

____

CONS OF THIS WEEK'S SKILL

____

____

____

WOO – HOO OF THE WEEK

____

____

____

____

REACTIONS TO THIS WEEK'S SKILL

____

____

____

____

____

____

____

____

DIFFICULTY OF SKILL

① ② ③ ④ ⑤ ⑥ ⑦

USEFULNESS OF SKILL

① ② ③ ④ ⑤ ⑥ ⑦

OVERALL MOOD THIS WEEK

NOTES

____

____

SOCIAL SUPPORT INVENTORY

This week you are asked to take inventory of your support resources such as the people, places, and professionals in your world that have your back.

- **Evaluate what types of support these individuals and resources can or do provide you.**
- **Include any details that may be useful later when feeling isolated and in need of support.**
- **Review and add or edit to the worksheets provided throughout this week.**
- **After completing the social support inventory ask yourself if there is an area that you could improve on.**
- **Over the next three months focus on increasing support in the areas you have identified as needing improvement.**

Building a support network is just as much of a coping mechanism as is deep breathing exercises, thought reframing, or journaling. The difference is a support network requires some maintenance and time to fully mature.

Social support comes from a variety of sources including, close family and friends/peers, healthcare providers such as doctors, counselors, patient advocacy groups, or support groups.

SOCIAL SUPPORT INVENTORY

Types of Support

Emotional Support:
- Provides love, understanding, and acceptance.
- Includes the expression of empathy, compassion, and caring.
- Usually found in our relationships with those closest to us but could also be an empathetic look from the customer next to you in line waiting just as patiently as you.

Informational Support:
- Provides advice, suggestions, and information, resulting in a growth of knowledge, mindset, and awareness.
- A more formal type of support, such as a healthcare provider, support group, or from a media resource.
- Instrumental support, which helps meet tangible needs. For example, a ride to a doctor's appointment or financial support or cooking a meal for someone.
- Provides a physical aide in some way.
- Typically service based.

Appraisal:
- Provides reassurance of your accomplishments.
- Provides you with the information for self-evaluation.
- Affirms your qualities.
- Found in words of affirmation, positive self-talk and encouragement, or a reward or recognition.

SOCIAL SUPPORT INVENTORY

RESOURCES FAMILY/FRIENDS/HEALTHCARE PROVIDERS/ INSTITUTIONS

My therapist, my neighbor . . . be specific with your list.

SOCIAL SUPPORT INVENTORY

WHO PROVIDES EMOTIONAL SUPPORT? AND HOW?

Spending an evening at my friend's house when feeling lonely.

WHO PROVIDES INFORMATIONAL SUPPORT? AND HOW?

Saw a video online that taught me how to use EFT for anxiety.

SOCIAL SUPPORT INVENTORY

WHO PROVIDES INSTRUMENTAL SUPPORT? AND HOW?

Jen from my support group offered to pick me up so I don't miss our meeting today.

WHO PROVIDES APPRAISAL TYPE SUPPORT? AND HOW?

My boss told me she really appreciates my dedication to the project.

REVIEW

PROS OF THIS WEEK'S SKILL

____

____

____

CONS OF THIS WEEK'S SKILL

____

____

____

WOO – HOO OF THE WEEK

____

____

____

____

REACTIONS TO THIS WEEK'S SKILL

____

____

____

____

____

____

____

DIFFICULTY OF SKILL

(1) (2) (3) (4) (5) (6) (7)

USEFULNESS OF SKILL

(1) (2) (3) (4) (5) (6) (7)

OVERALL MOOD THIS WEEK

NOTES

____

____

TAKE FIVE

Taking a five-minute break is a coping skill! Practice taking five-minutes a few times over the next week, at least three different times.

Take the time alone, without distractions; thus, no phones, laptops, or tablets, and no people . . . JUST YOU!!! If spending five-minutes still and silent sounds awful, then start with three minutes. Not a big deal, the goal is to work up to five-minutes.

When to Take Five:
- When feeling angry or in an argument with someone.
- When feeling anxious, overwhelmed, or confused.
- When you need to regroup yourself.
- Whenever you want a short break from life!

Where to Take Five:
- In your car before going into work or leaving work.
- Sitting on your porch or patio.
- In the shower or bath.
- On your couch in silence.

Benefits:
- *Helps regulate your mood and allows you to reconnect to yourself.*
- *Increases validation of your feelings and re-organizing of your thoughts.*
- *Helps in establishing and setting healthy boundaries.*
- *Increases self-awareness and self-respect.*

TAKE FIVE

Tips for Take Five:

- **Find a place of comfort and ease.**
- **Leave all electronics behind or at least silence them.**
- **Do not fixate on the five-minutes, just give yourself permission to be present and silent.**
- **If a thought comes, notice it, and remind yourself you can think about it in five-minutes if it needs re-examining.**
- **Try closing your eyes and just listen to the sound of your breath and feel the rise and fall of your chest as you inhale and exhale.**
- **Perhaps just let out three long exhales to help turn on the calming effects of your Vagus Nerve.**
- **Find a time of day that it is realistic to start practicing your five-minute break.**

*Learning to be alone with yourself encourages
higher levels of self-esteem, self-love, and self-compassion.*

REVIEW

PROS OF THIS WEEK'S SKILL

____

____

____

CONS OF THIS WEEK'S SKILL

____

____

____

WOO – HOO OF THE WEEK

____

____

____

____

REACTIONS TO THIS WEEK'S SKILL

____

____

____

____

____

____

____

____

DIFFICULTY OF SKILL

(1) (2) (3) (4) (5) (6) (7)

USEFULNESS OF SKILL

(1) (2) (3) (4) (5) (6) (7)

OVERALL MOOD THIS WEEK

NOTES

____

____

THE PROS AND CONS

Decision making can be a huge trigger for one's anxiety. And an oldie but a goodie is creating a pros and cons list to help weigh everything out before deciding. This week you will be using the pros and cons method to help in your anxiety management and decision-making processes.

Start by clearly identifying what you are deciding about. For example, "Should I pursue a new job or focus my efforts on the job I currently have?" Another example could be "Should I continue this friendship with _______?"

It is important to determine how timely the decision needs to be made. Give yourself a time limit on making the decision but keep it realistic.

When listing the pros and cons stick to the facts only, omit any opinions you or others may have.

Just because there are more pros then cons or the other way around does not mean that, that alone should be the reason you make the decision you decide. Remember one of those pros or cons may carry a lot of weight for you in the decision process.

If time allows you to revisit your pros and cons list so you can re-evaluate before making your final decision, then do so.

Benefits:
- *Speeds up the decision-making process.*
- *Allows you to see the whole picture from various perspectives.*
- *Provides a better understanding of the situation.*
- *Reduces indecisive behavioral patterns.*

THE PROS AND CONS

MAKE A LIST, CHECK IT TWICE!

REVIEW

PROS OF THIS WEEK'S SKILL

CONS OF THIS WEEK'S SKILL

WOO – HOO OF THE WEEK

REACTIONS TO THIS WEEK'S SKILL

DIFFICULTY OF SKILL

1   2   3   4   5   6   7

USEFULNESS OF SKILL

1   2   3   4   5   6   7

OVERALL MOOD THIS WEEK

NOTES

LAUGH YOUR WAY TO CHILL

This week identify three ways to intentionally make yourself laugh. A good laugh, full on belly type laughter. The type that makes you cry or catch your breath. After using humor to help calm down then revisit what may have been bothering you and see if your mind is in a more rational position to tackle the problem.

Most likely a friend or loved one has tried using humor to help you manage a difficult situation. And this moment of laughter or even a chuckle may have given you a reprieve to calm down slightly and regain some composure. That is the exact purpose of using humor as a coping skill.

Have you ever just been in a funk? Of course, you have, we all have. Ever watch your favorite comedy when feeling this way? What did it do? The comedy may not have rid you of your entire funk or the stressor you were experiencing but it probably gave you a break from the distressing experience and left you slightly less sad or overwhelmed.

LAUGH YOUR WAY TO CHILL

You have heard laughter is the best medicine, well it is in fact extremely beneficial to your physical and mental health.

Benefits:
- *Reduces stress and tension by stimulating your organs.*
- *Releases the feel-good neurotransmitters (dopamine, oxytocin, and endorphins).*
- *Laughter makes you smile which your body responds by releasing neurotransmitters which reduce stress.*

Laugh Your Way to Chill Examples:
- **Recall a memory that can't help but make you laugh so hard you could cry.**
- **Watch your favorite comedy show or movie.**
- **Look up videos on laughter yoga and give a session a try, laughter truly is contagious.**
- **Call a friend that is known to make you laugh and spend some time talking.**

THINGS THAT MAKE ME LAUGH

REVIEW

PROS OF THIS WEEK'S SKILL

____

____

____

CONS OF THIS WEEK'S SKILL

____

____

____

WOO – HOO OF THE WEEK

____

____

____

____

REACTIONS TO THIS WEEK'S SKILL

____

____

____

____

____

____

____

____

DIFFICULTY OF SKILL

(1) (2) (3) (4) (5) (6) (7)

USEFULNESS OF SKILL

(1) (2) (3) (4) (5) (6) (7)

OVERALL MOOD THIS WEEK

NOTES

____

HEALING ENVIRONMENT

This week you will be creating a healing environment for yourself in your own space.

Get creative and start with what you have. Make this a space that you want to go to, that you look forward to being a part of. A space to enjoy yourself even if it's only a few minutes a day.

Creating a healing environment can be an on-going coping mechanism and even part of a relapse prevention method. Part of adequate self-care is having a safe and comforting space for yourself daily. Providing yourself with a calming and nurturing space is a sign of self-worth and self-esteem. The point to this week's skill is to create something that is just for you within your home.

Benefits:
- *Increases feelings of relaxation and a sense of feeling grounded.*
- *Reduces anxiety, tension, and stress.*
- *Improves mindfulness skills.*

HEALING ENVIRONMENT

Healing Environment Example:

Placing big, comfy pillows or cushions on the floor in the corner of a bedroom. Hanging some small plants with LED lights strung through the hanging plants. Add your favorite affirmation and spirituality books nearby.

Another creative method is to change a spare room into a private library/tearoom, incorporate books, an electric fireplace and tea kettle, and of course an oversized comfy chair.

Personally, my favorite healing environment is the bathroom. Create a spa like experience as much as possible. Transforming an ordinary bath or shower into a luxury with aromatherapy, soothing colors, and upscale linens. This leaves me feeling relaxed and rejuvenated!

<u>QUICK TIPS</u>

- **Healing environments do not have to be extravagant.**
- **This space can be created on a budget with no problem.**
- **Create a small space that soothes you visually and physically.**
- **Use what you already have in your home environment.**
- **Keep your healing space free from clutter.**

HEALING ENVIRONMENT

HEALING ENVIRONMENT

What space do you have available for your healing space?

What items do you wish to add to this space?

Will you need to remove anything from this space? Are there items in the space that no long serve you?

What is the feeling you want this space to promote for you?

IDEAS FOR YOUR SPACE

- **Where** - *corner of a room, garage, shed, or even a dorm room.*
- **Comfort** – *beanbag chairs, oversized pillows, soft and fuzzy blankets, placed by a window for warm sunlight to shine on you.*
- **Aromatherapy** – *incense, candles, essential oils.*
- **Visual Enhancements** – *artwork, fresh plants, soothing lights.*
- **For The Ears** – *a sound machine, silence, soft music in the background.*

REVIEW

PROS OF THIS WEEK'S SKILL

____

____

____

CONS OF THIS WEEK'S SKILL

____

____

____

WOO – HOO OF THE WEEK

____

____

____

____

REACTIONS TO THIS WEEK'S SKILL

____

____

____

____

____

____

____

____

____

DIFFICULTY OF SKILL

(1) (2) (3) (4) (5) (6) (7)

USEFULNESS OF SKILL

(1) (2) (3) (4) (5) (6) (7)

OVERALL MOOD THIS WEEK

NOTES

____

A WHOLE LOT OF COPING

The bonus skill is making your own list of go-to coping skills. Skills that you can turn to when you are all out of ideas or feel so overwhelmed it is hard to think of what you can do in the moment. Feel free to add to the list already provided for you.

- Go for a Walk
- Go for a Drive
- Watch a Funny Video or Movie
- Spend Time with Friends/Family
- Spend Time with a Pet
- Play a Game
- Listen to Music
- Dance Like No One Can See You
- Journal
- Color in a Coloring Book
- Put a Puzzle Together
- Exercise – Run, Yoga, Weightlifting
- Use a Stress Ball or Silly Putty
- Read 5-10 Pages of a Book
- Make a Cup of Hot Tea
- Look Through a Photo Album
- Pop Bubble Wrap
- Watch the Clouds
- Draw a Picture
-
-
-
-
-

- Write a Gratitude List
- Ask for a Hug
- Take a Hot Bath or Shower
- Do an at Home Spa Day
- Read Positive Affirmations
- Get Outdoors
- Cook a Healthy Meal
- Call a Friend or Loved One
- Ride a Bike
- Take a Breath – Use Your Favorite Breathing Technique
- Focus on What You Can Control
- Learn a New Skill or Hobby
- Meditate
- Aromatherapy
- Listen to Binaural Beats for Calming
- Scream into a Pillow
- Go to a Local Park
- Count Backwards from 10
-
-
-
-

Woo-Hoo!

You did it! Congratulations, you have done more work on yourself than most!

If you have reached the end of this workbook, you now know what it is you are feeling and have allowed yourself to experience it without feeling out of control. You have more insight into what upsets you, the skills that soothe you, and behavioral patterns that no longer serve you.

All this insight and self-awareness is what leads to the ability to "own who you are." By learning to "own it," as I like to call it, you have the power to grow and evolve into the individual you wish to be. So, continue to keep yourself calm, own your stuff, and trust in who you are!

Keep on Coping,

Tara Arhakos

www.mindfulmomentsllc.com
@TaraArhakos

APPENDIX

MEDITATIONS
&
EDUCATION SHEETS

SCRIPT FOR BREATH OF FIRE

- Start by finding a comfortable seat in which your spine is tall. Ideally cross legged on the floor, placing your palms facing up on your knees. If you have a cushion or yoga block this may help with your posture. Focus on keeping your chest up and open, creating space from your belly button to your heart.

- Slowly inhaling through the nose and out through the mouth. Now repeat this breath two more times, taking a slow deep inhale through the nose and exhaling through the mouth. Now breathing normal, roll the shoulders back and down so you start to feel your rib cage come closer to your body in a neutral like state. Allow your facial muscles to relax as you start to close your eyes or find a spot on the floor as a focal point.

- Start slowly until you find a bit of comfort with this pattern. As you start to get comfortable you will find the rhythm takes over. You can choose to place one hand on your belly if this helps with performing the breath work.

- Begin to inhale through your nose and feel your belly expand and press into the hand laying on top of it. Then exhale with a snap of the abdomen so your hand quickly moves back in towards your spine. Repeat this pattern while keeping the inhale and exhale at the same pace and length.

Continued on next page

SCRIPT FOR BREATH OF FIRE

- As you continue to inhale and exhale, release any hold in between and make it a continuous cycle of breath. If it helps visualize the cycle of oxygen in through the nose going into the belly and circling right back around to exhale through your nose. As you become more comfortable with the Breath of Fire the inhale becomes more passive and just cycles into the exhale.

- Notice your spine and the engagement of your core. Focus on using the abdominal region to help press the breath out. With each snap of the stomach the breath releases quickly from your body.

- As you feel the heat buildup in you and the energy begins to ignite, allow your mind, body, and breath to connect and become one in this moment. Repeat the Breath of Fire four more times before you begin to end your practice.

- As you start to come to the end of your practice you will take a deep inhale through the nose and exhale through your nose. Return to your natural breath placing the palms back on your knees face up or you may place them on your stomach.

- Allow yourself to sit quietly and just notice any changes within your body from this activity. Do you feel more grounded? Is there a spark of energy flowing through you now? Does your mind feel more at peace? Just notice whatever is happening in your body and psyche at this time. No judgment is necessary about any of these sensations. They are not good nor are they bad, just notice them for what they are.

- When you are ready you can slowly open your eyes and bring your awareness back to the room.

SCRIPT FOR BODY SCAN MEDITATION

Start by finding a comfortable seat or lying down. Start to feel your body fully connected to the surface you're either lying down on or where you are sitting. Feeling your feet firmly against the ground, feeling your seat supported by the chair underneath you. Closing your eyes gently and slowly start to listen to the sound of your breath. Feel the rise and fall of your chest as you naturally breathe in and out.

In a moment you will start to go through each body part just noticing any sensations within your body. Noticing any tension or pain, noticing any relaxation, and doing this without judging the sensation that you notice. In fact, you may notice no sensation at all, which is completely okay. If your mind starts to wander at any point in time during this body scan just notice that it wandered and bring your attention back to the body part that you're focusing on.

Taking a deep breath in through your nose and exhaling through your mouth and return to your natural breath. Starting to bring your awareness to your toes just noticing any feelings that you might be having in your toes. And just saying to yourself in your mind, I notice that my toes feel *and fill in the blank*. Now slowly moving onto your feet and just noticing any sensation that may come to you in this moment that's coming from your feet. Again, just saying to yourself I notice my feet feel, may be sore. And just noticing that sensation.

Continued on next page

SCRIPT FOR BODY SCAN MEDITATION

Now moving up to your calves and shins and spend some time here noticing any feelings or sensations that come from this area of your body. Rising from your calves to your hamstrings and just noticing any tightness that may be there or any tingling sensations that might come to you. And just saying to yourself I notice my hamstrings feel and fill in the blank.

Bringing your awareness slightly upwards to your buttocks and notice any sensations that you may feel at this time. Continue onto your lower back, the midback to the upper back. Just noticing any feelings that come about as you travel from the lower portion of your back to the upper back. Take notice of any tension, tightness, or other sensations in these areas.

Now rise to your shoulders. The shoulders are often a place that tension is held, so take notice of anything that you might be feeling in this area. Moving from your shoulders to your chest, notice any sensation there, any tension, any tightness or perhaps there's no feeling at all. While here at your chest, notice your breath. Notice if it's deep with slow exhales or if your breath is shallower. Just repeat to yourself I notice my breath *and fill in the blank*.

Slowly bring your attention to your abdomen, the abdominal area is often very susceptible to physical symptoms of stress and anxiety. So, just notice with your mind any sensations that you can feel within your stomach.

Continued on next page

SCRIPT FOR BODY SCAN MEDITATION

Start to bring your awareness to your fingertips, noticing any sensations that might be within your fingertips. Travel to the length of your fingers and feel each individual finger for itself. First on the left hand and then on the right and just create awareness of any of the sensations that you may experience at this time in your fingers.

From your fingers notice your palms into the wrists, from your wrists noticing any sensations in the forearms and then traveling into your biceps. And again, consciously aware of any sensations that you may have come across as you traveled from your fingertips up to the top of your arms.

Now your attention may have wandered, gently remind yourself that this is perfectly normal and okay and just bring yourself back to the meditation and the body part that you're focusing on.

Finally, you're going to bring your awareness to your neck and just notice any tension or stiffness that may be lying there. Traveling from your neck you're going to bring your attention to your face and all the facial muscles. Notice if your forehead is scrunched or if it's relaxed. If your brow area is constricted or not.

Notice if your eyes are closed tightly or if they're more gently closed. Notice your mouth and any sensations around your lips. Any tingling sensations or tension? Are you frowning or is your mouth natural?

Continued on next page

SCRIPT FOR BODY SCAN MEDITATION

Notice your jaw, another area tension is often held. Is your jaw tightening? Notice any tension around your mouth and your jaw. Just sitting in these sensations for a moment allowing yourself to take inventory of what you have felt thus far as you start to move your attention to the last and final body part.

Focusing your attention on your head, just take notice of any sensations that you feel at the top of your head on your scalp. You may feel a tingling sensation, you may feel nothing. There is no right or wrong sensation to have here. Anything that you notice just in this moment.

Know that any of these sensations that you've experienced can change at any given time throughout your day or throughout this meditation. Taking an inhale through your nose holding it at the top and just thinking of all the feelings that you felt through this meditation letting out a big exhale through the mouth and release all those sensations you have just experienced.

Allowing yourself to return to your natural breath, breathing in through the nose out of the nose. Feeling the rise and fall of your chest again slowly, start to bring your awareness back to the room. Maybe wiggling your fingers and your toes to start. Slowly rolling your wrist one way and then the other and doing the same with your ankles. You might point and flex the feet. You may start to gently shake out the hands and when you are ready roll the shoulders forwards and back.

Continued on next page

SCRIPT FOR BODY SCAN MEDITATION

Start to slowly open your eyes and bring your awareness back. Knowing that you can always come back to this body scan when you start to feel disconnected from yourself whether that's physically or emotionally.

The mind body connection aids in the ability to regulate our feelings and take ownership of our emotions and our emotional state. I thank you for allowing me to be your guide during this personal and physical journey.

SCRIPT FOR WHAT IS YOUR BODY TELLING YOU?

Create a comfortable space on the floor for you to lie down and connect to the Earth. Breathing in through the nose and slowly exhale through the mouth. Bring your attention to the rise and fall of your chest as you allow your breath to naturally create its own pattern. Focus on the sensation of your back being completely supported by the ground beneath you.

As you start to feel the sensations within your body begin to take a slow mental scan from your toes through your mid-section, into your arms, over your shoulders and into your scalp. Even take a moment to scan for any sensations within your ears. Just noticing any experiences in your body. Notice these sensations without judgment.

Take a deep breath into the belly and exhale through the nose. Now bring your awareness to those sensations that you discovered during your scan. Ask those sensations what has brought them about? Ask them why they have decided to reside in this part of your body?

For instance, you may ask your shoulders what is this tension trying to tell me? Or you may ask the twinging feeling you found in your left foot what has brought you here?

Begin to connect the sensations to the emotions. Allow yourself to ask, what does my body feel like when I feel worried? How does my body respond to anxiety or anger? What areas are more likely to ache when I am feeling depressed?

Continued on next page

SCRIPT FOR WHAT IS YOUR BODY TELLING YOU?

Just allow yourself to contemplate these questions. No answer is necessary at this moment, but if one comes to you just take note of it for yourself. In a moment you will bring your attention back to the room and be asked to journal about this experience.

Bring your attention back to your breath and the sensation of the Earth beneath you. Slowly inhale and exhale. Bring one hand to your heart and the other to your belly as you continue to breath naturally. Rolling over to one side, keeping the eyes closed. Placing one hand down to the Earth and slowly coming up to a seated position. Just breathing here for a moment and when you are ready, start to flutter the eyes open.

Without hesitation quickly write whatever came up during and after the meditation practice. As always there is no right or wrong answer to this experience. You may include what you discovered physically or emotionally or both. This is just to be used as a reference for you. As you practice getting to know your physical – emotional connection more intimately you will find patterns and themes.

END STINKING THINKING

UNHELPFUL STYLES OF THINKING

- <u>All or Nothing</u>: Thinking in extremes. Black and white thinking or all or nothing. Usually the words always or never are in these thoughts.
  - *Example: I'm never invited to lunch at work.*

- <u>Overgeneralizing</u>: Taking one event or occurrence and applying it to all or in general.
  - *Example: After failing one math test you conclude that you are just horrible at math.*

- <u>Mind-Reading</u>: To assume that you know what other people are thinking.
  - *Example: You knock an orange off the display at the grocery store and believe everyone must be looking at me thinking I am such a loser that can't even pick out an orange without making a mess.*

- <u>Fortune-Telling</u>: When you predict what the outcome will be. Typically, people predict a negative outcome of an event or often you may find yourself predicting what someone will say to you in a conversation before even having the conversation.
  - *Example: "I'm not going to get the job." or "Why bother asking? I know exactly what she will say."*

Continued on next page

END STINKING THINKING

UNHELPFUL STYLES OF THINKING

- <u>Catastrophizing or Minimizing</u>: To catastrophize, like fortune-telling, is when you assume the worst possible outcome will happen even from the smallest incident. Minimizing on the other hand is downplaying the severity of a situation. Minimizing can often be seen in substance abuse when the person using is in denial.
  - Example: I only drink a glass or two after work and then on the weekends I let myself have a little more.

- <u>Mental Filter</u>: This is simply discrediting the positive.
  - *Example: You receive your annual review, and your supervisor tells you that you are doing a great job at most things but points out that you are consistently late coming back from lunch by 5 minutes. After this you can only focus on the one piece of negative feedback and neglect all the positive feedback you received.*

- <u>Emotional Reasoning</u>: *This happens when you are interpreting your world through just your feelings. As if the lens you are looking through is "I feel _____ therefore it is/ I must _____."*
  - *Example: Walking down the street you feel anxious and think to yourself "I feel anxious I must be in danger."*

Continued on next page

END STINKING THINKING

UNHELPFUL STYLES OF THINKING

- <u>Should/Ought/Must Statements</u>: This thinking style creates strict and rigid expectations of oneself, others, and the world. These statements often cause unrealistic expectations leading to anger, frustration, and disappointment.
  - *Example: "I should lose 10 pounds before I see my family for the holiday." "My husband should know I don't want to go on vacation in August."*

- <u>Personalization</u>: You blame yourself for things that are not your fault or are out of your control. Personalization may also happen when you believe you are being targeted or deliberately ignored by someone. You may feel victimized at times when experiencing this style of thinking.
  - *Example: A mother blames herself for allowing her child to go to a party, who is then hurt in a car accident on the way home. "It's my fault, if I had not said yes to him going to the party he would not have gotten hurt on the way home." Another example of personalization is when a friend is discussing their belief around diet and exercise and you take it as a personal attack on your own diet and exercise routine.*

SCRIPT FOR ROOT TO RISE GROUNDING

Start by finding a comfortable seat. One in which you can have both feet placed flat onto the ground. Sitting up tall and gently closing your eyes or finding a focal point for yourself.

Slowly inhaling through the nose and letting it out through the nose. Allowing your breath to become natural. Begin bringing your awareness to your feet. Feel the ground beneath the balls of your feet and your heels connected to the surface beneath you. Focusing on the energetic connection between yourself and the support of the ground.

Bring your awareness to your sit-bones. Feel your sit-bones begin to connect fully to the cushion beneath you. Feel the cushion conform to your sit-bones. Breathing in and breathing out.

Raise your awareness to the trunk of your body, the core. The part of your body which keeps you upright and secure. The dependable part of you that is so easy to take for granted. Breathing in feel the rib cage hug into the body, zipping the ribs up tightly. Exhale while engaging the abdominals to feel more upright. Start to feel the spine straighten slightly.

Focus on the chest expanding. Inhale, bring the shoulders up to your ears and exhale rolling them down the back. Feel the sturdy base you have created thus far. Inhale through the nose and exhale through the nose.

Continued on next page

SCRIPT FOR ROOT TO RISE GROUNDING

Finally bring your awareness to the crown of your head. Imagine there is a string attached to the crown of your head that is slowly pulling you toward the sky. Expand your spine, vertebra by vertebra, while keeping your head neutral. Inhale and exhale.

Feel the length of your tailbone to the tip of your head. Feel the heaviness that rests from your sit-bones down to your feet. Inhale for a count of three, 1 – 2 – 3 and exhale for 3 – 2 – 1. Repeating this sequence four more times.

Inhale 1 – 2 – 3, exhale 3 – 2 – 1.
Inhale 1 – 2 – 3, exhale 3 – 2 – 1.
Inhale 1 – 2 – 3, exhale 3 – 2 – 1.
Inhale 1 – 2 – 3, exhale 3 – 2 – 1.

Now inhale into the belly, another small inhale into the chest. And exhale with a sigh through the mouth. Sitting here in this moment just notice any sensations you may be experiencing. Return to your natural breath. And begin to wiggle the toes, wiggle the fingers. Roll the neck side to side. And slowly bring your awareness back, opening your eyes when you are ready.